# Easy-to-make
# TABLES
# & CHAIRS

By the Editors of Sunset Books
and Sunset Magazine

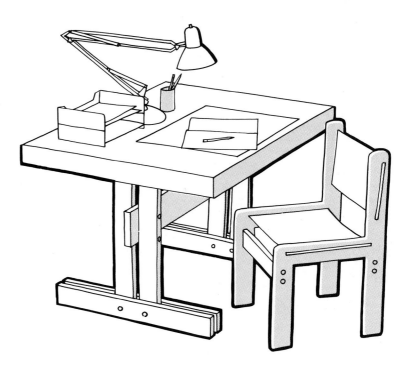

Lane Publishing Co., Menlo Park, California

**Surviving four centuries,** *old Spanish trestle table has maintained its design integrity from past to present. This classic's contemporary counterpart — shown on the front cover — is discussed fully on page 42.*

With a little help from our friends . . .
A book that involves so many elements of research, building, testing, photography, and writing gathers participating friends along the way.

For their ideas and help in gathering information and making prototypes, we thank Steve Coffee, The Furniture Makers, The Just Plain Smith Company, Lynne Morrall, Bill Provost, Victor Tobolsky, Roberta Vandervort, and all of the project designers.

And for their generosity, our thanks to George Dean of *Mobilia* and to the *Jordan International Company.*

## Edited by Donald W. Vandervort

### Design and Illustrations: Ted Martine

#### Photography: Norman A. Plate

Cover: Directions for trestle table on page 42; birch chair directions on page 34.

Editor, Sunset Books: David E. Clark

Ninth printing March 1984

# Contents

# A WORD ABOUT
# THIS BOOK...

You need furniture, right? Relax. Though buying new furniture can destroy a well-planned budget, by making pieces yourself you can keep expenses under control, explore a craft, and enjoy the satisfaction of creating.

*Easy-to-make Tables and Chairs* focuses on the two most needed kinds of furniture in a home. Projects include coffee tables, dining tables, dining chairs, easy chairs, couches, lounges — and more. You'll find an assortment of materials, styles, and degrees of simplicity. Flip through to see the variety.

You can brush aside any doubts you might have about your skill as a craftsman. If you can swing a hammer, saw off a board, or thread a needle, you have creative potential. With good plans, step-by-step guidance, and a little time, anyone can fashion pride-inspiring furniture.

Tools? You can get by with fewer than you might expect. All projects feature a "bare minimum tools" schedule that lists the necessities. But don't make the job tougher than it needs to be. Tools can determine whether a project is easy or difficult to make. The right tools pay off — a luxury such as a $15 saber

With their elements of contemporary design, simplicity, comfort, and, in most cases, low cost, these table and chair projects are designed for you. They reflect plain materials, honestly used. As the maxim says, "honesty is integrity." Where bolts can easily form a strong joint, bolts are used. In the same spirit, clear finishes on most projects enhance the wood's natural coloration.

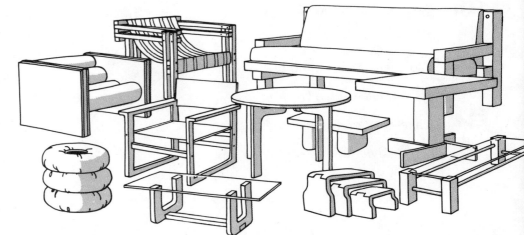

saw will greatly simplify making many projects.

Consider tools an investment. Your savings from not buying furniture should more than cover tool expenses, and you'll have tools next time you need them. (Hopefully, there *will* be a next time.)

### How to get the most from this book

Projects and the techniques to make them — these are what this book offers you. Pages 6 through 65 contain 35 table and chair projects shown in color and accompanied by complete directions. Supplementary how-to information, beginning on page 66, rounds out the book.

So glance through until you find something that appeals to you. Though project types are not divided by clear boundaries, the projects tend to flow through the book in a certain order. First are lounges, followed by couches and groupings, easy chairs, straight chairs, dining tables, and small tables. Most projects group in twos or threes under a common title and introduction, according to their common traits. The introduction tells a little about each.

Following each introduction, the how-to-do-it instruction begins. Before starting a project, read through these directions. Included are lists of the tools you'll absolutely need ("Bare minimum tools"), the tools that can simplify your work ("Helpful tools"), and the necessary materials ("Materials to buy"). Step-by-step directions ("Here's how") guide you through all the processes in simple terms and with helpful sketches.

To devote maximum space to projects and necessary information, project directions avoid repetition. General information and techniques needed for making several projects are presented in the section beginning on page 66. Turn to these pages when you want detailed information on buying materials, using tools, mastering joinery techniques, making cushions and slings, finishing, and the general "ins" and "outs" of making tables and chairs.

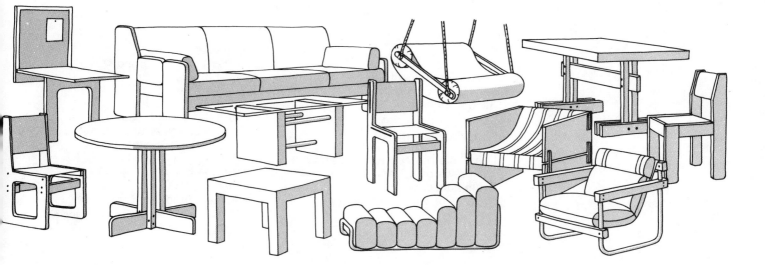

# FABRIC-COVERED FOAM: SOFT & COZY

Can you handle a needle and thread? If sewing is your forte, this furniture is for you. No muss, no fuss, no sawdust.

Take some foam chunks or polystyrene beanbag pellets, give them shape and a fabric skin, and suddenly — seating. And not just ordinary seating, but seating that is fun, decorative, and very comfortable.

The three designs shown owe their comfort to foam stuffing and modular styling. The foam squishes to meet your contours — you can shift the cushions around until they form the shape of seat or lounge you want.

**The caterpillar lounge,** for example, is a series of seven cushions held in a tubing frame. You can interchange the cushions to form the curve that fits *your* curves. Cushions are simply chunks of foam covered with drawstring-type covers. The frame that holds them together is made from bent, mild-steel tubing that's been chromed. To provide this you can either have mild-steel tubing bent at a muffler shop and then chromed or you can make the frame from something else — like 2 by 2s or painted electrical conduit.

**The wall-to-wall cushions** are just large, knife-edge cushions held in place by the room walls. You can arrange them however you want them — even flat on the floor for overnight guests.

**The backbone beanbag** is just what its name implies: a beanbag divided by vertebra-style sections. Hang it on the wall as a large graphic, fold it up as a seat, or spread it out for lounging.

# Caterpillar lounge

*Colorful cushions are interchangeable for ultimate comfort.*

(Photo on facing page)

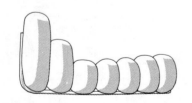

**Bare minimum tools:**

Pencil
Measuring tape
Compass
Hacksaw

Drill
Bit: ¼ "
Sewing equipment, sewing machine
Serrated bread knife
Steel wool

**Materials to buy:**

Foam in sizes and densities shown
  in drawings 8-1 and 9-2
Foam adhesive
15 yards of cotton upholstery
  cording

1 yard blue fabric
1⅝ yards medium orange fabric
⅝ yard purple fabric
⅝ yard red fabric
⅝ yard yellow fabric
⅝ yard light orange fabric
Matching polyester threads
13' of ⅞ " i.d. mild-steel tubing
8' of ⅞ " o.d. mild-steel tubing
8 machine bolts, ¼ " by 1¼ " with
  washers and nuts
Paint (see directions for frame)

*(Continued on page 8)*

## Caterpillar lounge

*See facing page*
*Design: Stephen L. Coffee*

## Backbone beanbag

*See page 9*
*Design: Roberta Vandervort*

## Wall-to-wall cushions

*See page 8*
*Design: Pamela Pennington,*
   *Pennington & Pennington*

. . . Continued from page 6

## Material notes:

Use 1 by 1 rib-knit jersey of cotton, acrylic, or blend of fibers that will stretch widthwise 75% (10" will stretch to 17½"). This fabric is sometimes sold for cuffs or T-shirt and sweater necklines.

## HERE'S HOW:

Begin by cutting and gluing together the foam pieces according to drawing 8-1 and the information on page 78.

Next, make the drawstring-type covers (more about making these on page 80). First, preshrink the fabric. Then cut out each cover following the patterns shown in drawing 9-1.

Fold the fabric in half crosswise with the right sides together. Sew ½" seams joining the two halves along their sides, using a zigzag or stretch stitch, stretching the fabric slightly as it goes through the machine. Leave what will be the bottom of the cushion unsewn. If using a straight-stitch machine, sew two parallel rows of stitching for extra strength.

Turn each cover right side out and put it on its foam to check for fit. If it doesn't fit snugly, remove it and sew wider seams.

Now turn under the bottom edges of the cushion cover ½" and press.

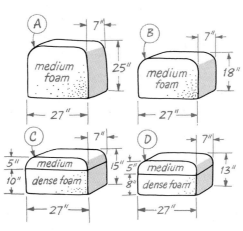

DRAWING 8-1
FOAM CONSTRUCTION

Turn under another ½" and pin them in place. Stitch all the way around, leaving room for a drawstring and leaving about 2" unsewn at the center of one side.

Remove the pins and fish the cording into the casing (first tie one end of the cording to a safety pin). Leave 6" of the cord hanging out each end of the casing, turn the cover right side out, and slip it over the foam. Pull the drawstring tight and tie it, tucking the extra cord ends inside the cover. Repeat this process for the remaining covers.

Last, make the frame. At a muffler shop, have the tubing bent into the form shown in drawing 8-2. Join the two bent ends with the straight tubing by cutting it to length,

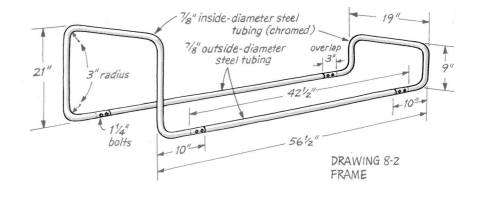

DRAWING 8-2
FRAME

# Wall-to-wall cushions

*Stack large cushions between the walls to fill your room with seating.*

(Photo on page 7)

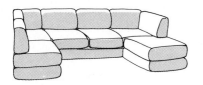

### Bare minimum tools:

Pencil
Measuring tape
Sewing equipment, sewing machine

### Materials to buy:

Because the amounts of materials necessary for this project depend upon the size of your room and the number of cushions you will make, fabric quantities cannot be accurately listed.

### HERE'S HOW:

Measure your room and lay it out on graph paper to figure how many and what size cushions you need.

All pieces are from 8" foam, wrapped once in each direction with polyester batting and stuffed into a knife-edge cover (see page 79 for information on making knife-edge cushions). The bottom cushion — one long length under the main portion of the seating — is dense foam. The individual seat cushions and back wedges are medium foam.

Make cushions the heights and depths shown in drawing 9-3;

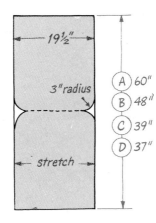

DRAWING 9-1
FABRIC DIMENSIONS

pushing the end pieces onto it, and drilling holes for ¼" bolts.

Remove the ends, polish them with steel wool, and paint them or take them to a plating shop to have them plated with bright nickel. Also paint the straight tubing. Using bolts, reassemble the frame, put the cushions in place, and relax on your new caterpillar lounge.

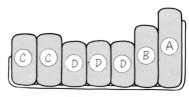

DRAWING 9-2
CUSHION ARRANGEMENT

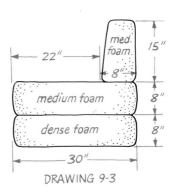

DRAWING 9-3

figure the lengths according to your room size.

Order foam cushions and back wedges cut to size (look under "Rubber — Foam and Sponge" in the Yellow Pages).

# Backbone beanbag

*This jointed beanbag lies flat, folds, bunches... even hangs from the wall.*

(Photo on page 7)

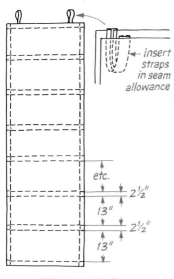

## Bare minimum tools:

Yardstick
Sewing equipment, sewing machine

## Materials to buy:

7 yards of 36" wide fabric*
Matching thread
3 cubic feet of shredded foam
3 cubic feet of polystyrene pellets
1 dowel, ½" by 36"
Two medium screw hooks

*Denim is a good choice. Use striped fabric or piece together two colors to make the stripes (for piecing, use 45" wide fabric).

## HERE'S HOW:

This beanbag is basically a long, thin, knife-edge cushion that has eight divisions sewn across it (knife-edge cushions are discussed on page 79).

Begin by cutting two 36-inch-wide fabric panels 10' 2½" long and, for the straps, two fabric strips 3" by 6".

To make the straps, fold the fabric strips in half lengthwise with right sides together. Allowing for ½" seams, stitch along the top and side. Turn the right side out. Press. Fold in half crosswise.

Now with right sides together, join the large panels with pins along the top and two sides. As you work, insert the straps into the seam allowance, each 4" in from the sides along the top edge, as shown in drawing 9-4. Be sure to match the stripes.

Sew along these three seams, stitching through all layers. Remove the pins and turn the bag right side out. Press.

On the fabric, mark stitching lines, using tailor's chalk and a yardstick. The cushions are 13" long, separated by 2½" dividers.

Pour into the bag a mixture of half foam and half pellets until the mixture approaches the first stitching line (since working with pellets can be messy, consider doing this step in the garage or outside). Pin or baste across the stitching line; then sew, forming the first of eight cushions.

Sew along the second stitching line, forming the 2½" divider. Then continue this process — filling, sewing, sewing, filling — until all eight cushions and seven dividers are formed. Sew the bottom seam closed by turning in the raw edges and top stitching.

**Alternate method.** Another way to make the beanbag is to first stitch the two ends and one side and then sew the dividers across the tube. Fill all pockets; then hand or machine stitch the remaining side closed. This way, it's easier to refill the pockets if the pellets go flat.

DRAWING 9-4

**Softwood coffee table**
*See page 13*

**4-by-4 couch**
*See facing page*
*Design: Richard Stamm*

# BOLT-TOGETHER COUCH, MATCHING TABLE

What's easier than cutting off boards and bolting them together? That's the kind of simple construction that characterizes both the couch and coffee table shown here. Because they are both easy to make and inexpensive, these projects are ideal for beginning woodworkers who would like to fill voids in their living rooms or family rooms.

Standard softwoods make up almost the entire set. Though the couch and table shown were made from finished redwood, you could substitute fir or cedar.

## 4-by-4 couch

*Standard 4 by 4s form this couch's basic framework.* (Photo on facing page)

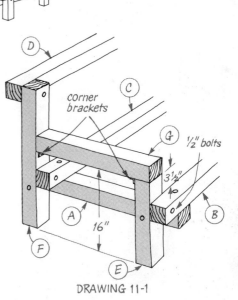

**Bare minimum tools:**

Pencil
Measuring tape
Square
Drill
Bit: ½", ⅝", #6 by 1¼" and
  #8 by 1½" pilots
Adjustable wrench
Screwdriver
Hammer
Serrated bread knife
Sewing equipment
Sandpaper and finishing tools

**Helpful tools:**

Stapling gun
Radial-arm saw
Drill press
Power sander
Electric carving knife

**Materials to buy:**

40' of 4 by 4
11' of 2 by 4
2' by 8' of ⅝" plywood or particle
  board
12' of ⅛" by 1" pine edging
14 carriage bolts, ½" by 8" with
  washers and nuts
4 corner-angle brackets, 2½" by 3"

28 screws, 1¼" by #6
14 screws, 1" by #6
14 screws, 1½" by #8
4 nylon leg glides
4 joist hangers for 2 by 4s
1 foam slab 3" by 22½" by 72"
2 foam slabs 4" by 26" by 72"
6 yards upholstery fabric, 54" wide
100' nylon sash cord
White glue
Tape or brads
Clear polyurethane sealer
Clear polyurethane finish

**HERE'S HOW:**

Begin by cutting, or having the lumberyard cut, the following lengths:
(A) Two 4 by 4s, 33⅜"
(B,C,D) Three 4 by 4s, 79"
(E) Two 4 by 4s, 16"
(F) Two 4 by 4s, 29¼"
(G) Two 4 by 4s, 26⅜"
(H) Two 2 by 4s, 64½"
(I) One ⅝" plywood or particle
  board, 22½" by 71"
According to drawing 11-1 and detail drawing 11-2, mark, fit, drill, and bolt together the (A,B,C) frame pieces — but don't tighten down the

*(Continued on next page)*

**DRAWING 11-1**

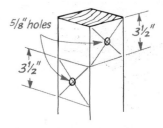

5/8" holes
3½"
3½"

DRILLING LAYOUT FOR A,B,C
DRAWING 11-2

. . . Continued from page 11

nuts. Measure and mark the four legs (E,F), drill the holes, and bolt them in place. Tighten the twelve nuts gradually, going from one to another and back several times, allowing the structure to get rigid without getting cockeyed. Add the (D) support. Then secure the arm (G) with corner brackets and 1¼" screws.

Next center marks and drill ½" holes every 3" along (C) and (D) as illustrated in drawing 12-1. Thread the sash cord through the holes, first knotting it at one end and then pulling it tight as you thread.

Using sandpaper, round off sharp corners and remove any irregularities on the frame. Wipe on a coat of penetrating sealer. Let it dry; then follow with two coats of satin polyurethane finish.

Fasten the 2 by 4s (H) to the bottom surface (I) using glue and 1½" screws, driving the screws through (I) into (H). Push the

assembled support into the frame with the 2 by 4s facing down as shown in drawing 12-2. Temporarily fasten it there, using tape or brads.

Turn the frame onto its back, push the joist hangers onto the 2 by 4s, and fasten the hangers to the (A) pieces with 1¼" screws. By not nailing the 2 by 4s to the hangers, you can easily remove the seat support when upholstering it.

Use a serrated bread knife or an electric carving knife to trim the 3" foam slab to the seat support's size. Save the large scraps. Set a second 4" foam slab on the first slab, letting it overlap the front cross beam (B). See the cushion support detail (drawing 12-3).

Position the remaining foam block against the back cords between the rear legs, resting on top of the seat cushion. Trim it slightly oversize, saving the large scraps. Insert all of the long scraps between the back foam block and the cords to give the cushion fullness.

Now the back and seat each receive fabric (see drawing 12-4). Cut the fabric into two pieces, each 3 yards long. Tack one long edge of one piece to the front side of (D). Secure it by mounting an edging strip with 1" wood screws.

Stretch the fabric over and around the back cushion and down across the front edge of the rear cross beam (C). Pull it tight at the center and tack or staple it to the bottom of the beam, working from the center to the sides. Tack the fabric sides to the insides of the rear legs (F).

Cover the bottom cushion identically, mounting an edging strip on top of (B) and tacking the fabric's ends and back underneath the cushion support. Trim with scissors as you tack.

Drill holes in the bottom centers of the feet and tap in the furniture glides.

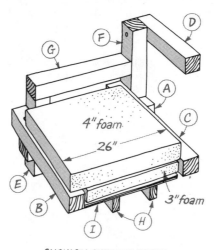

CUSHION SUPPORT DETAIL
DRAWING 12-3

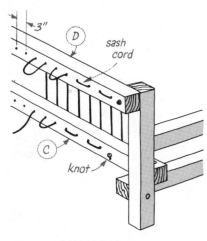

DRAWING 12-1

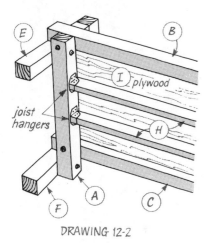

DRAWING 12-2

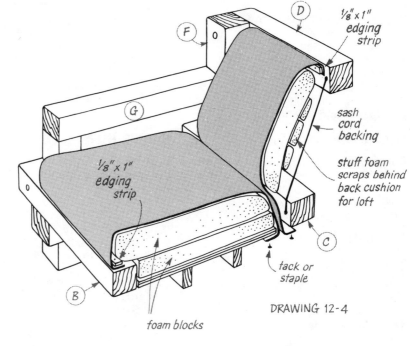

DRAWING 12-4

# Softwood coffee table

*You can make this easy coffee table in half a day.*

(Photo on page 10)

## Bare minimum tools:

Pencil
Measuring tape
Square
Handsaw
Hammer
Nailset
Screwdriver
Drill
Bits: ½", #10 by 2" pilot
Sandpaper and finishing tools

## Helpful tools:

Radial-arm saw
Drill press
Power sander

## Materials to buy:

(A) 5' of 4 by 4
(B,C,D) 30' of 1 by 4
(E) 3' of 1 by 2
4 carriage bolts, ½" by 4½"
4 washers and nuts, ½"
8 flathead screws, 2" by #10
Small box each 6d, 3d finishing nails
White glue
Clear polyurethane sealer
Clear polyurethane finish

## HERE'S HOW:

Begin by cutting the various boards to the following lengths (use a square to mark and check your cuts):
(A) Four 4 by 4s, 14"
(B) Seven 1 by 4s, 34½"
(D) Three 1 by 4s, 17"
(E) Two 1 by 2s, 16"

Lay the five top pieces (B) upside down on a flat surface, first arranging them for grain, color, and knot pattern. Using 3d nails and glue, nail the (D) crosspieces across them; put one 1" from each end and one across the center.

Measure the distance across the top, add 1½", and cut the two (C) ends to length. These should be about 19" long.

Assemble the (B) and (C) frame pieces with glue and 6d nails, using the top as a guide for keeping the (B,C) frame pieces square.

Next, attach the legs (A), screwing them from the inner sides of (B) using two 2" screws per leg. Mark the outside face of each 4 by 4 leg for its ½" hole, centered 1¾" down from its top end. Drill the holes and insert the carriage bolts. Add washers and tighten on the nuts.

Hold the table top in the frame at its proper level and mark for the 1 by 2s (E) that support it. Remove the top; then glue and nail (with 3d nails) those 1 by 2s in place. Reposition the top and glue it to the 1 by 2s.

Sand off corners and irregularities; then wipe on one coat of penetrating sealer. Let it dry. Finally, add two coats of clear finish.

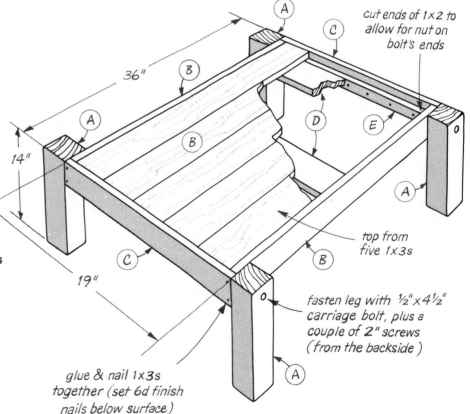

cut ends of 1x2 to allow for nut on bolt's ends

36"

14"

19"

top from five 1x3s

fasten leg with ½"x4½" carriage bolt, plus a couple of 2" screws (from the backside)

glue & nail 1x3s together (set 6d finish nails below surface)

# EARTHY BUT ELEGANT SET

Earthy, elegant warmth: that's the feeling you'll get from these oak furnishings.

The take-apart couch — a bolted-together oak frame that holds cushions in a sling — offers 7' of comfort. The ottoman serves as a luxurious footrest and doubles as an extra seat. And though the large coffee table's intricate herringbone surface looks as if it were created by a master craftsman, it's surprisingly easy to make from oak flooring. The three pieces form a set, but you don't have to make all three. They work well as singles.

## Oak and leather couch

*Knock-down solid oak frame cradles cushions in a canvas sling.*

(Photo on facing page)

### Bare minimum tools:

Pencil
Measuring tape
Square
Compass
Coping saw
Hacksaw
Table saw
Drill
Bits: 1/8", 5/32", 3/16", 1/4", 3/8", 11/16", countersink
Doweling jig or tool for cutting spline slots
Bar or pipe clamps, C-clamps
Wrenches
Mallet or hammer
Router, 3/4" radius, 1/4" bits
File
Sandpaper and finishing tools
Sewing equipment, sewing machine

### Helpful tools:

Saber saw
Radial-arm saw
Drill press
Power sander

### Materials to buy:

(A,B,C) 12' of 1¾" by 9½" oak
(D) 7' of 1⅜" by 6" oak
(F,G) 7' of 1⅜" by 2" oak
(E) 7' of 1⅜" by 5¼" oak
(H) 7' of 1⅜" by 1⅜" oak
2' by 8' sheet of ¼" hardboard
2' of 1" by 1" angle iron
1' of flat aluminum bar, 1" by ⅛"
4 dowels, 4' by ⅜"
12 hanger bolts, washers, and nuts, 5/16" by 2"
10 hanger bolts and nuts, ¼" by 2"
4 screws, 1¼" by #8
4 flathead screws, 1½" by #8
3 flathead screws, 1" by #8
12 flathead screws, 1" by #10
Resorcinol resin glue
6 yards of 36" wide canvas
1 medium foam slab, 2" by 22" by 7'
1 medium foam slab, 2" by 24" by 7'
2 soft foam slabs, 2" by 22" by 7'
2 super-soft foam slabs, 2" by 24" by 7'

1 medium foam block, 4" by 24" by 2' (arms)
2 cans of foam adhesive
11 yards of 36" wide fabric

### HERE'S HOW:

Begin by cutting (or having the dealer or a cabinetmaker cut) the various pieces to size, according to the following dimensions. Mark and check all cuts with a square. Cut carefully. Refer to drawing 17-3.
(A) Two 1¾" by 9½" by 30" oak
(B) Two 1¾" by 9½" by 20¾" oak
(C) Two 1¾" by 9½" by 16" oak
(D) One 1⅜" by 6" by 84" oak
(E) One 1⅜" by 5¼" by 84" oak
(F,G) One 1⅜" by 2" by 84" oak
(H) One 1⅜" by 1⅜" by 83¾" oak
One 23" by 82" by ¼" hardboard

Next, cut the 1-inch-radius corners specified in drawing 16-1, (next page) using a coping saw or saber saw. Also cut the angle across the back legs (A). Using the router and a ¾" radius bit, round all edges on all boards. Clamp them down firmly as you work.

Now spline or dowel the (A,B,C) sides together. (For information on

*(Continued on page 16)*

**Herringbone table**

*See page 16*

**Generous ottoman**

*See page 17*

**Oak and leather couch**

*See facing page*

*Group design: Don and Roberta Vandervort*

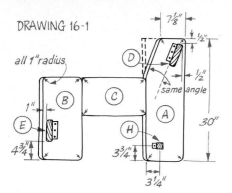

DRAWING 16-1

all 1" radius

placements of the rail brackets according to drawing 16-1. Drill ¼" pilot holes for 5/16 by 2" hanger bolts; then drive in each hanger bolt (see page 73).

Be sure each bracket slides easily onto its hanger bolts. If it doesn't, slightly enlarge the bracket's holes.

When all 5/16" hanger bolts are installed, remove the brackets (remembering which goes where) and set them on the rails (D) and (E), as shown in drawing 16-2.

Drill ⅛" holes 1" deep for 1" by #10 screws; then screw the brackets to the rails.

Have someone help push the rails' brackets onto the hanger bolts. Add washers and nuts and snug down the nuts.

Now make the canvas clamp-down supports (F) and (G). Rip the 1⅜" by 2" piece at an angle, as shown in drawing 16-3. Notch the ends of (F) and (G) to fit around the brackets and bolts. Then bolt one half to the (D) rail and one half to the (E) rail (see drawing 16-3) using five ¼" by 2" hanger bolts each, countersinking the nuts below the surface in an 11/16" hole.

The bar (H) that joins the two back legs (A) is secured to the legs at each end by a 2¾" piece of 1" aluminum bar. Two 1½" by #8 screws, countersunk in the bar,

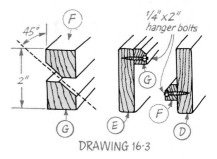

DRAWING 16-3

fasten it to (H). Then two 1¼" by #8 screws, countersunk in the other side of the aluminum, screw the bar to each back leg (A). Drill ⅛" pilot holes in the wood.

Go on to make the sling (see page 77 for information on sewing slings). Because the needed width of fabric is not commonly available, cut three 6' lengths of 36-inch-wide fabric and join their edges, using flat-fell seams. Finish all edges. Leave the end casings unsewn.

Sand all wooden parts until sufficiently smooth; then apply two coats of clear, penetrating polyurethane finish. Let the first coat dry before you apply the second one.

Hold one of the long edges of the sling just the way it will curl over (G) and poke a hole through it at one end, where a hanger bolt is. Work your way across the front, repeating this process. Push (G) onto the

making these joints, see page 74.)

Make the metal brackets for the rails (D) and (E) from angle iron, according to drawing 16-2. Using a hacksaw, cut them to length, file corners and rough edges, and drill the holes (or buy predrilled iron).

When the sides (A,B,C) are dry, remove the clamps and mark

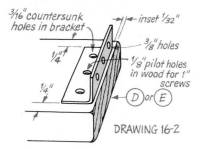

³⁄₁₆" countersunk holes in bracket

inset ¹⁄₃₂"

⅜" holes

⅛" pilot holes in wood for 1" screws

(D) or (E)

DRAWING 16-2

# Herringbone table

*(Photo on page 15)*

## Bare minimum tools:

Pencil
Measuring tape
Square
Table saw or router
Drill
Bit: #10 by 1½" pilot
Mastic spreader
Screwdriver
Bar or pipe clamps
Sandpaper and finishing tools

## Materials to buy:

(A) 16 sq. ft. of 5/16" flooring
(B) 4' by 4' sheet of ½" plywood
(C) 16' of ¾" by 3" oak
(D) 6' of 5/4" by 8" oak
Wood flooring mastic
White glue
12 flathead screws, 1½" by #10
Detergent
Wood paste filler (natural or oak)
Clear polyurethane finish

## HERE'S HOW:

First make the top from wood parquet flooring (A) glued to a plywood base (B). This 5/16-inch-thick flooring comes in precut, prejoined blocks, normally about 1 foot square, with a paper backing.

Without using mastic, lay out the blocks on the plywood base, paper backing facing up. Arrange the wood grain and coloration for best appearance. Then pick them up, remembering where they go.

Prepare a bowl of lukewarm water and detergent. Thinly spread on the mastic according to the label directions. Lay the blocks in place, paper side up, aligned with the plywood's straightest edge, tight fitting and in straight rows.

Dip a rag in the detergent water and scrub the backing off the tiles. As you do this, hand fit them all snugly together. When you finish this process, lay a flat board on top, place a heavy object on the board, and let the mastic dry overnight.

The next day you can trim off the edges. To duplicate the table size shown, cut the top to 41" by 41¾". Be sure all corners are a true 90°.

Fill all of the gaps and cracks, using a wood paste filler (available at the flooring dealer). Sand off the

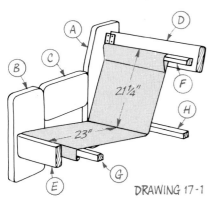

DRAWING 17-1

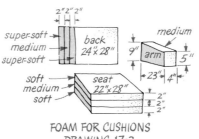

FOAM FOR CUSHIONS
DRAWING 17-2

hanger bolts and cinch it down. Mark along the underside of (G) for the casing that holds 3/8" dowels (casings along both edges of the sling are optional if you cinch down (G) and (F) tightly).

Set the hardboard on the seat part of the sling. Now have a helper raise the sling until it is at the approximate measurements given in drawing 17-1. Screw the front edge of the hardboard to (G), with 1" by #8 screws, flush with the seam between (G) and (E). Repeat the sling-fastening procedure, adjusting measurements as you go.

If you wish, remove the sling and make casings for the 3/8" by 3 1/2' dowels.

Last, make the cushions. As you can see in drawing 17-2, the seat

and back are composed of three 2" layers of foam. Glue the 7' slabs together with foam adhesive; then divide them into thirds.

The covers are the knife-edge type discussed on page 79. They have folded miter corners (see page 80).

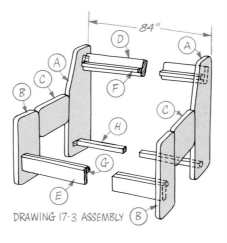

DRAWING 17-3 ASSEMBLY

excess by hand. Then either belt-sand the top until flat and smooth or, for a minimal charge, take it to a planing mill or large lumberyard to have it run through a drum sander.

Next cut the groove in the frame pieces (C), according to drawing

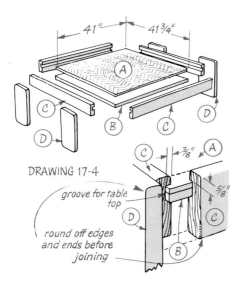

DRAWING 17-4

groove for table top

round off edges and ends before joining

17-4, using a router or table saw.

Round the four outer edges of the (C) pieces, using a router and 3/8" quarter-round bit or using sandpaper. Then get the exact length for these from the top. If your top is exactly the same size as the one shown, these (C) pieces will be 41 3/4" and 41" (two each.) Cut them to length and round off their top edges and ends, as shown in drawing 17-4.

Be sure the (C) pieces fit properly around the top; then glue and clamp them with two bar or pipe clamps going each direction. Wipe off excess glue.

Cut the legs (D) to 16" and round all edges. Use a square to mark and check your cuts.

When the glue is dry, remove the clamps and turn the framed top upside down on a flat surface. Glue and screw each leg in place, flush with the table's top edge and side.

Fill and sand; apply two coats of penetrating polyurethane finish.

# Generous ottoman

(Photo on page 15)

## Bare minimum tools:

Pencil
Measuring tape
Square
Table saw or router
Drill
Bit: #10 by 1 1/2" pilot
Screwdriver
Bar or pipe clamps
Sandpaper and finishing tools
Sewing equipment, sewing machine
Serrated bread knife

## Helpful tools:

Router
Radial-arm saw
Power sander
Electric carving knife

## Materials to buy:

(A) 4' by 4' sheet of 1/2" plywood
(B) 10' of 3/4" by 3" oak
(C) 5' of 5/4" by 8" oak
12 flathead screws, 1 1/2" by #10
White glue
Clear polyurethane finish
1 medium foam slab, 4" by 2' by 3'
1 2/3 yards of 36" wide batting
1 2/3 yards of 36" wide fabric
Matching thread

## HERE'S HOW:

Because the ottoman frame is made the same way as the coffee table frame discussed at left, follow the directions given for the coffee table, modifying the dimensions to those shown in drawing 17-5. Just skip over the part about making the wood flooring top. Make the cushion like the couch cushions, cutting the foam block to 24" by 29 1/2".

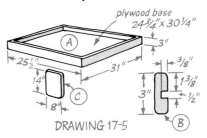

DRAWING 17-5

## Balloon chair

*See facing page*
*Design: Loyd C. Moore, Design Fore*

## Inner-tube seats

*See page 21*
*Design: Don Vandervort*

# BOUNCY, AIR-FILLED SEATS

If you have a sense of humor, you might like to try air-filled seating. It bounces, squishes, and cozily conforms to your body. Air-filled seats are strong enough to flop on, yet light enough to toss about. (If you have cats, though, these seats aren't for you — one slip of the claw and the better part of this furniture could disappear.)

Shown here are a balloon chair and inner-tube seats. Both are put together from everyday materials, using nothing more sophisticated than inner tubes, balloons, cardboard, tape, and fabric. Material costs are very low (ask tire stores or gas stations for secondhand inner tubes and repair the leaks).

Making **the balloon chair** requires no special talents — just a strong pucker and a healthy set of lungs (or a pump). But these chairs are only temporary. Balloons usually stay inflated for a couple of weeks but may begin to shrink after that. You can prolong a chair's life by keeping a few spare balloons handy for refilling.

**Inner tubes** come in all sizes. Experiment to find comfortable combinations by tying them together; look at a few possible variations in the photograph. The covers — cylinders of fabric with drawstrings at each end — fit most standard sizes of tubes, but you can modify them to create unusual shapes.

# Balloon chair

*Colorful and comfortable, this temporary chair stars at parties.*

(Photo on facing page)

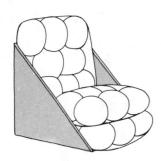

**Bare minimum tools:**

Pencil
Ruler
Scissors

**Materials to buy:**

20″ by 23″ by 23″ cardboard box
35 sq. ft. 4-mil polyethylene
1 roll of 10-mil polyethylene tape
About 3 dozen large, quality
  balloons

**Material notes:**

Buy unmarked boxes at moving companies or pick up free boxes from appliance dealers and decorate them.

Polyethylene is cheapest by the roll. You could also try containing the balloons with thick garbage bags or with fabric. Fabric feels better to sit on, but a fabric cover has to be sewn and you can't see the balloons through it.

Clear and colored plastic tapes are available at home-improvement centers. Hot-air heating duct tape works, too.

*(Continued on next page)*

... Continued from page 19

## HERE'S HOW:

To begin, cut, score, and fold the cardboard box as shown in drawing 20-1. Extra-thick cardboard doesn't

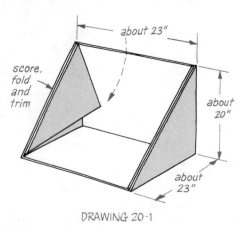

DRAWING 20-1

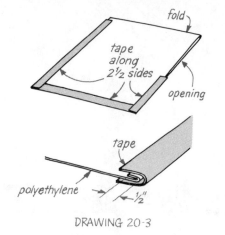

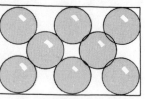

DRAWING 20-3

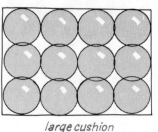

small cushion

large cushion

LAYOUT OF BALLOONS
DRAWING 20-4

need to be folded for strength.

Next, make the cushions. If the box's size is different from the example, modify cushion dimensions to fit it. Lay out and cut

In order to make the balloons last longer, don't fully inflate them. Just fill them until they are firm. Stuff them into the cushions, distributing them as shown in drawing 20-4. You'll need eight 10" balloons for the small cushions and twelve 10" balloons for the large cushion.

Keep the cushions pressed flat so they are 10" thick. The covers should fit tightly. When all balloons are inside, finish taping the cushions closed.

Drawing 20-5 shows how to tape the cushions together. Assemble the

two seat cushions first; then tape them to the back. Just set the group of three cushions in the box frame. To prevent the cushions from sliding out, you can tape the bottom cushion to the box or spray adhesive on the bottom cushion and in the box.

Once the chair is finished, you're ready to test it. As you prepare to sit, you'll probably wonder if it can really hold you. Sit with confidence. If made properly, it won't let you down.

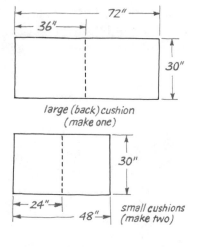

DRAWING 20-2

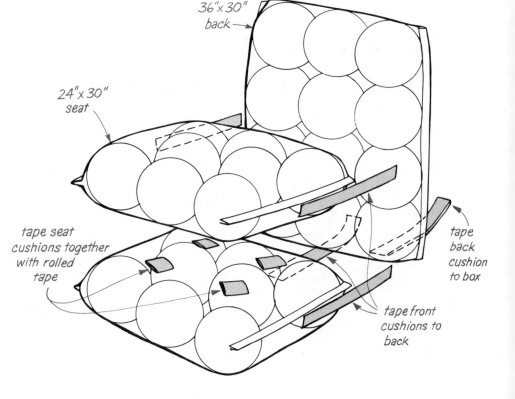

DRAWING 20-5

the polyethylene according to the pattern given (see drawing 20-2). Fold each length in half and tape the edges together, leaving a gap for stuffing in the balloons (see drawing 20-3).

When you tape, fold over about ¼" of both sheets so the tape won't touch the balloons once they are inside. Trim off ½" of two corners to allow air to escape.

# Inner-tube seats

*Inner tubes and a cloth cover— that's all you need.*

(Photo on page 18)

### Bare minimum tools:

Pencil
Measuring tape
Sewing equipment, sewing machine
Pump (gas station)

### Materials to buy:

Inner tubes
Fabric*
Heavy, colored cord

*Choose heavy, durable fabric. Amount depends upon number and size of tubes (see directions below).

### HERE'S HOW:

Begin by inflating the inner tubes. Fill them full — but not so full that they lose their sponginess. Wash them if they're dirty and repair any leaks (tube-repair kits are available from auto-supply stores).

Stack the tubes to form a seat. Experiment. If you make a seat with a back (like the blue and green one in the photograph), tie the tubes together with heavy cord or cotton rope before you add the cover. (That chair's back tube was deflated slightly, doubled back, and tied.)

Next, make the cover. Because it can be drawn tightly to fit, its dimensions are not critical. It's better to be too loose than too tight.

Measure the circumference of the seat's main tubes, adding a couple of inches (see drawing 21-1). That's the length of fabric you'll need. Width depends upon the seat's

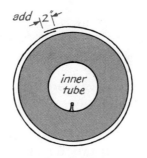

DRAWING 21-1
DIMENSIONS OF COVER FABRIC

height. Measure the stack's height, add the largest tube's diameter, and add 2 inches for seams (see drawing 21-2). That's the proper fabric width. Cut the fabric to size or piece extra widths accordingly.

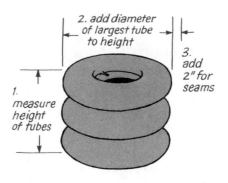

DRAWING 21-2
FINDING WIDTH OF FABRIC COVER

Lay the fabric right sides together, folding its length in half. Sew the two ends together and press the seam open. Then sew a ½" casing for drawstrings along both edges, leaving a ½" opening for inserting the drawstring. (See more about making this kind of cover on page 80.)

Work the drawstrings through the casings. Do this by tying a large paper clip or safety pin on each cord's end and pushing it through.

With the cylinder wide open, cut and knot the drawstrings' ends. Pull one drawstring fairly tight and push the inner tubes into the fabric from the other end. Then cinch up both

DRAWING 21-3

drawstrings. Wrap another string outside the cover between the inner tubes, cinching tightly to stretch the cover and show off the tubes' forms.

DRAWING 21-4

# EASY-TO-MAKE BUDGET CHOICES

Wandering through a lumberyard trying to meet the demands of a Tolstoy-length materials list isn't much fun. It's even less fun when you get to the check-out counter. If you've ever experienced this, you'll probably appreciate the simplicity of these two chair designs.

One chair has a framework made entirely from 2 by 2s; a single sheet of plywood makes the pair of chairs. Both designs utilize canvas and foam rubber for comfortable seating. Add the fasteners — and that's it.

The shop work is almost as easy as the footwork. Making the chairs is simple; you use only a few basic tools. Just cut out the pieces and fasten them together.

**For the plywood chairs,** practically any ¾″ plywood works well. If you'll place the chairs outdoors, choose exterior-grade plywood. Otherwise, choose standard A-A plywood and paint the chairs like the ones shown. Or try a high-quality hardwood-veneered plywood and finish them naturally. If you plan to paint them, you might like to try using density-overlaid plywood — it has flat, smooth surfaces that take paint exceptionally well.

**For the 2 by 2 chair,** buy softwood 2 by 2s or — if you feel like using something slightly more extravagant — buy birch, ash, or some other hardwood milled to standard dimensions. Remember that a 2 by 2 is not 2″ by 2″ — it is milled to 1½″ by 1½″.

# 2-by-2 lounge chair

*Strong lines and simple construction characterize this easy-to-make casual chair.*

(Photo on facing page)

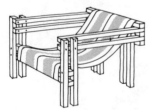

## Bare minimum tools:

Pencil
Measuring tape
Square
Handsaw
Hammer
Drill
Bits: ⅜″, 1″
Wrench
Sewing equipment
Sandpaper and finishing tools

## Helpful tools:

Radial-arm saw
Rasp
Hacksaw (otherwise have rods cut)
Socket wrench
Sewing machine

## Materials to buy:

40′ of 2 by 2
2 yards of 30″ wide canvas
1 length of 1″ dowel (for plugs)
16 carriage bolts, ⅜″ by 2½″
4 carriage bolts, ⅜″ by 4″
2 threaded rods, ⅜″ by 7″
24 washers and nuts, ⅜″
Small box of upholstery tacks
Foam slab, 1″ by 3′ by 1′
White glue
Clear polyurethane finish

## HERE'S HOW:

Using a square to mark the lines and check for accuracy, begin by cutting the various pieces to the following lengths:
(A,B) Six 2 by 2s, 29″
(C) Three 2 by 2s, 26″
(D) Four 2 by 2s, 24½″
(E) Four 2 by 2s, 23″

Next, countersink the ⅜″ bolt holes 1″ with a 1″ bit where washers and nuts will go. First mark their placement, centered ¾″ from each side of the 2 by 2. Holes specified at ends of 2 by 2s are ¾″ from the ends. Where they occur in pairs, they are 3″ apart.

Assemble the pieces with carriage bolts and threaded rods as illustrated in drawing 24-3.

*(Continued on page 24)*

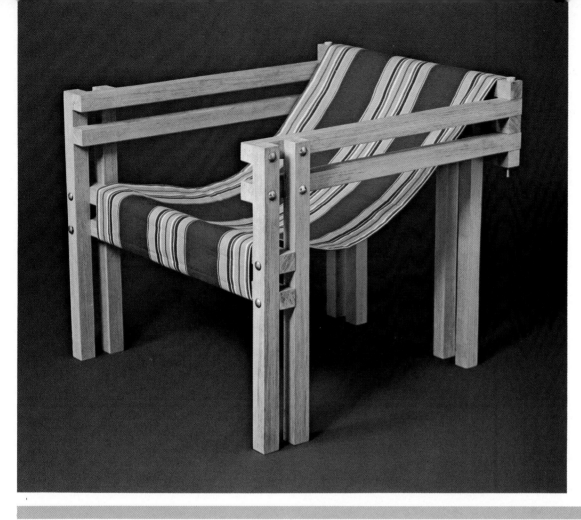

**Pair of plywood chairs**

*See page 24*
*Design: John S. Clark*

. . . Continued from page 22

Pound ¾" dowel plugs into the countersunk holes as shown in drawing 24-1 and sand them flush. (Those plugs over the heads can be glued.)

Round the top edges of the front and back cross-supports (B,C), and tack a length of foam rubber along them to add softening. Sand the wooden parts and apply two coats of clear polyurethane finish.

plug

countersink 1" hole 1" deep for nut and plug

DRAWING 24-1

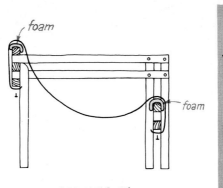

foam

foam

DRAWING 24-2

Make the sling as described on page 77. Tack it in place as shown in drawing 24-2, adjusting it to the proper curvature. You may want to add a cushion to the back for comfort.

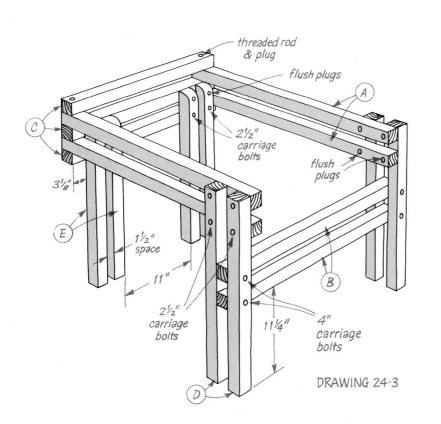

threaded rod & plug

flush plugs

C

A

2½" carriage bolts

flush plugs

3⅛"

E.

1½" space

11"

B

2½" carriage bolts

11¼"

4" carriage bolts

D

DRAWING 24-3

# Pair of plywood chairs

*For indoors or out, these chairs are inexpensive, durable, and—most of all—easy to make.*

(Photo on page 23)

## Bare minimum tools:

Pencil
Measuring tape
Handsaw
Hammer
Sewing equipment
Sandpaper and finishing tools

## Helpful tools:

¾" chisel
Saber saw
Table saw
Sewing machine

## Materials to buy:

4' by 8' sheet of ¾" A-A plywood
4 yards of 30" wide canvas
Small box of upholstery tacks
Foam slab, 2" by 1' by 3'
Paint or other finish

### HERE'S HOW:

Start by marking the cutting lines on the plywood, according to drawing 25-1. Be sure to allow for the saw blade's width ("kerf") when marking the pieces.

Cut the slots to the size illustrated in the detail (drawing 25-2) by making several passes with a power saw or by making two cuts, then chiseling out the wood in between. Sand or file them smooth. Do this work carefully; if the slots are too long, the chair's pieces won't fit together properly.

Narrow the top edge of the pieces labeled (E) so the seat's front edge will be 15¾" from the floor (see drawing 25-3). Fill, sand, and paint.

For a very sturdy chair, glue the pieces as you assemble them. Otherwise, assemble them without glue; this way you can disassemble the chairs for storage and moving.

The seat is simply a canvas sling (see how to make sling seats on page 77). If you wish, you can add cushions for comfort.

To soften the chair's front and back edges, you'll do well to tack lengths of dense foam rubber along the top edges of pieces (D) and (E) beneath the canvas. In providing for comfort, the angle of the sling is critical. Though drawing 25-5 shows how to attach it, don't fasten it permanently to the lower edge of the piece labeled (D) until you have it right. You may have to vary the amount of slack. Don't expect too much comfort from the arms; they're a bit too thin.

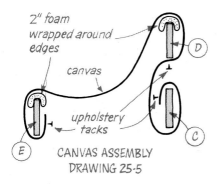

CANVAS ASSEMBLY
DRAWING 25-5

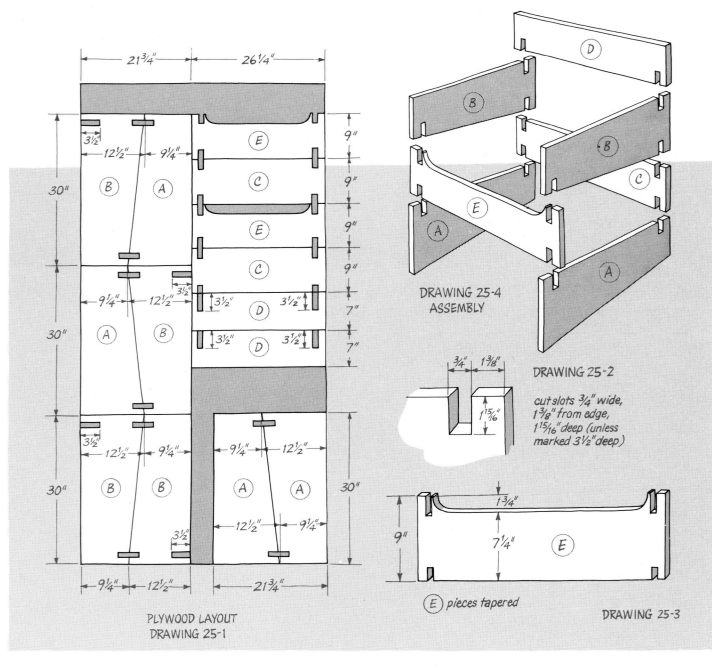

PLYWOOD LAYOUT
DRAWING 25-1

DRAWING 25-4
ASSEMBLY

DRAWING 25-2

cut slots ¾" wide, 1⅜" from edge, 1¹⁵⁄₁₆" deep (unless marked 3½" deep)

DRAWING 25-3

(E) pieces tapered

**Hanging leather & ash chair**
*See facing page*
*Design: Norman A. Plate*

**Tête à tête swing for two**
*See page 29*
*Design: Rick Morrall*

# SEATING THAT SWINGS & SWAYS

Novel, romantic, fun — these are words that describe a hanging chair. Both of the chairs shown here are reasonably easy to put together (the foam-roll one is a breeze). Make one and you'll discover just how special a hanging chair is. As you drift and sway, you'll learn that a hanging chair is more than just comfortable — it's the essence of leisure.

There's only one problem; you may have to wait in line for your turn.

**The modern, slung-leather chair** is designed to be kept under cover. It's made from ash, doweling, rope, and leather (you can use canvas instead of leather). Ash or a similar hardwood works best; softwoods can be used only if the dimensions are enlarged to add strength. The chair hangs from a stiff garage door spring bought at a junkyard.

**The foam-roll lounge** costs less and is considerably easier to make. Despite its simplicity, it is remarkably comfortable — especially for two. It is made from a pair of foam rolls with dowels poked through their centers; the rolls are held at each end by a length of birch and ropes. Each foam roll is enclosed in a canvas tube, and a large canvas sling fits slackly from roll to roll. The lounge can be used either outdoors or indoors.

# Hanging leather & ash chair

*Hang it from a beam or a tree limb—then sway away the day.*

(Photo on facing page)

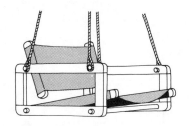

**Bare minimum tools:**

Pencil
Measuring tape
Square
Hammer
Drill

Bits: ¼", ½", 1¼"
Handsaw
Coping saw
Sandpaper and finishing tools
Leather-cutting tools

**Helpful tools:**

Band saw or saber saw
Radial-arm saw
Drill press
Doweling jig
Router with quarter-round bit
Power sander

**Materials to buy:**

(A,B) 12' of 1¾" by 2¾" ash
(C) 5' of ¾" by 2½" ash
(D) 3' of ¾" by 5½" ash
(E) 3 hardwood dowels, 1¼" by 3'
(F) 1 hardwood dowel, 1¼" by 18"
(G) 1 hardwood dowel, ½" by 3'
(H) 1 hardwood dowel, ¼" by 4'
Latigo leather: 40" by 16", 40" by 22"
20' to 40' of rope
Heavy spring (optional)
Small box upholstery tacks
Large eyebolt (optional)
Resorcinol resin glue
Wood filler
Clear polyurethane finish

*(Continued on next page)*

. . . Continued from page 27

## HERE'S HOW:

Start by cutting the pieces to size. Use a square to mark and check your cuts; work as precisely as possible. (See page 69 for more information on cutting.)
(A) Four 1¾" by 2¾" ash, 27"
(B) Four 1¾" by 2¾" ash, 8½"
(C) Two ¾" by 2½" ash, 29"
(D) Two ¾" by 5½" ash, 18"
(E) Three dowels, 1¼" by 31"
(F) Two dowels, 1¼" by 3"
(G) Fourteen dowels, ½" by 2"
(H) Sixteen dowels, ¼" by 3"

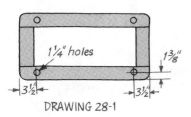

DRAWING 28-1

Next, dowel together the side frames, using two ¼" dowels per joint. (Find more information on dowel joinery on page 74.)

Then drill the 1¼" holes for the connecting dowels where shown in drawing 28-1. Drill until the drill bit protrudes from one side; then finish from the other side. This way you won't split the wood.

The pieces labeled (D) in drawing 28-2 are made by first drilling the 1¼" hole centered 9" from each end and 3" from one edge and then by drawing and cutting the curve, using a band saw, saber saw, or coping saw. The curve is basically a 1¾" radius. Mark the ½" radii of the various corners and cut them at this time, too.

Then drill the 1¼" holes in the two pieces labeled (C).

The next main job is rounding and shaping all of the edges. A router with a quarter-round bit can do much of the work in a hurry, but if you don't have one, you can do all of the work by hand with sandpaper. Sand all of the edges and corners until they are pleasantly rounded. This is the time to do finish sanding on all of the surfaces.

Join the various parts of the chair by pushing them onto the 1¼" dowels (you may have to sand the ends of the dowels slightly). Mark for placement of the ½" dowel pegs. Then drill the ½" holes for them, sliding the 1¼" dowels back and forth slightly to allow the drill unobstructed access. Be sure the pegs at each end of each dowel are parallel with each other.

Cut the shorter 1¼" dowels for the top corners of the arms. Spread a little glue on them and insert them in place. Sand the inside surface flush with the arm; then drill and add ½" dowel pegs. Complete all the sanding on the chair and add a clear polyurethane finish.

Now for the leather. Cut out the back shape according to the pattern (drawing 28-3). Wrap it all the way

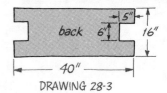

DRAWING 28-3

around the (D) pieces and tack it to the edges that face forward, first removing the ½" dowels and pushing the (D) pieces together. Put on the leather seat, a 22" by 40" rectangle, the same way.

Eye-splice or loop and tie four ropes to the four dowels as shown in the photograph. Either tie them directly to a beam or tree or tie them to a stiff spring and hang the spring from the support.

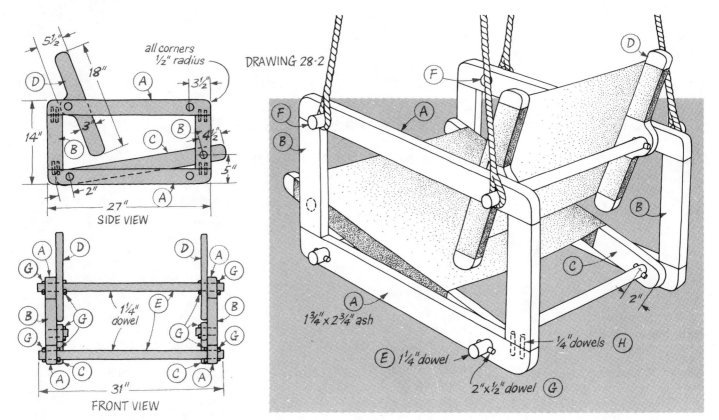

DRAWING 28-2

SIDE VIEW

FRONT VIEW

# Tête à tête swing for two

*This peg-together lounge is made without nails, screws, or glue.*

(Photo on page 26)

## Bare minimum tools:

Pencil
Measuring tape
Saw (or have pieces precut)
Drill
Bits: ½″, 1¼″
Sandpaper and finishing tools
Sewing equipment

## Helpful tools:

Sewing machine

## Materials to buy:

(A) 6′ of ¾″ by 2″ birch
(B) 2 dowels, 1¼″ by 4′
(C) 2 polyurethane foam rolls,
8″ by 36″ with center
    holes predrilled
1⅔ yards of 41″ wide fabric
2⅔ yards of 36″ wide chair canvas
Polyester threads that match the
    fabric and canvas
2 pairs of long shoelaces
Twine
About 30′ of ⅜″ rope
2 large eyebolts
Clear polyurethane finish

## Material notes:

If you're not able to find foam rolls (bolsters) with holes drilled through them, you'll have to modify the method of inserting the dowels. In this case cut the rolls in half — lengthwise — with a bread knife or electric carving knife. Then lay the dowel down the center and glue the two halves back together with foam adhesive.

## HERE'S HOW:

Begin by cutting the framework pieces. Cut the boards (A) to 36″ lengths and cut the dowels (B) to 41″. Round the corners of (A).

Drill 1¼″ holes centered 1½″ from each end of the frames (A).

Then drill a ½″ hole 1″ from each end of the dowels. Add a clear finish to the frames.

Push the dowels through the foam rolls (see "Material notes"). Then make the drawstring covers for the foam rolls. For each, stitch a piece of fabric to make a tube 41″ long and 26″ around, and add a casing at each end (see more about making drawstring covers on page 80). Use the shoelaces for drawstrings.

Wrap the 8′ by 3′ canvas around the two tubes, adjust for proper slack, mark it, and then double stitch the ends together (as shown in drawing 29-1). Turn to page 78 for more on making this kind of sling.

Add the frames (A) to the sides and knot the ends of the ropes through the ½″ dowel holes. Loop the other ends through eyebolts in porch rafters or around a tree limb. Once you find a comfortable angle, set the chair's pitch by lashing the ropes together with twine.

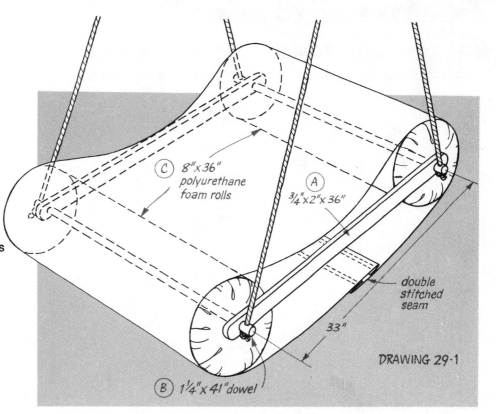

(C) 8″x 36″ polyurethane foam rolls

(A) ¾″x 2″x 36″

double stitched seam

33″

DRAWING 29-1

(B) 1¼″x 41″dowel

# BIG CHAIRS, BOLD COMFORT

You might never think of car mufflers and garage door springs in connection with furniture. Yet both these materials make up parts of the two chairs shown here. A garage door spring supports one of the foam-roll cushions in the chair at upper right, and the tubing framework of the other chair was bought and bent at a muffler shop.

The oversized **foam roll chair** is actually large enough to seat two. Its width is determined by the fact that garage door springs come only in a limited number of lengths; the shortest length you can find will dictate the chair's width. Construction is simple. Cylindrical foam bolsters are held at the proper seat angle by two box sides. The sides shown are covered by ¼″ mahogany panels; you could choose other panels or even wrap fabric around standard ¼″ plywood.

**The muffler-pipe chair** has a basic framework of bent steel tubing joined with ash; cushions sit on a canvas sling that's stretched between the wood supports. Considering its large size, this chair is relatively lightweight. By removing six bolts, you can disassemble the entire frame into flat pieces.

# Foam roll chair

*Four foam cylinders provide surprisingly comfortable seating; the bottom one springs to fit your contours.*

(Photo on facing page)

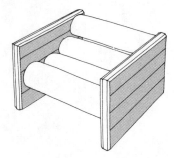

## Bare minimum tools:

Pencil
Measuring tape
Square
Handsaw
Drill
Bits: 3/16″, ¼″
Hammer
Nailset or small nail
Adjustable wrench
Sandpaper and finishing tools
Serrated bread knife
Sewing equipment

## Helpful tools:

Table saw
Clamps
Electric carving knife
Sewing machine

## Materials to buy:

(A) ½ sheet (4′ by 4′) of ⅝″ plywood
(B) 1 sheet of ¼″ veneer, 4′ by 8′
(C, D) 20′ of 1 by 3 pine
(E) 22′ of ½″ by 3¾″ oak threshold
4 hardwood dowels, 36″ by 1¼″
1 garage door spring, 9-gauge by 28″
4 cylindrical foam bolsters, 8″ by 30″
8 lag bolts, ¼″ by 3½″
2 eyebolts with nuts, ¼″ by 3″
10 washers, 1½″ diameter, ¼″ hole
4 rubber leg tips
4 yards of 36″ wide fabric
Matching thread
4 yards of 36″ wide batting
White glue
1 box of 5d box nails
1 box of 1″ brads
Wood filler
Clear polyurethane finish

(Continued on page 32)

## Foam roll chair

*See facing page*
*Design: Rick Morrall*

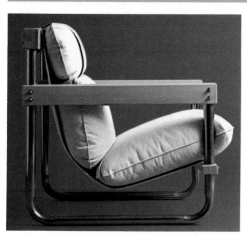

## Muffler-pipe chair

*See page 32*
*Design: Don Vandervort*

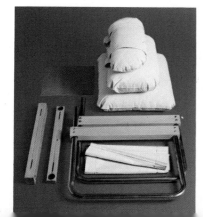

. . . *Continued from page 30*

## HERE'S HOW:

Making the box frames is a good place to start. Refer to drawing 32-3. Use a square for marking and checking all cuts. For the two sides, cut the following:

(A) Two 24" by 36" panels and ten 3" by 6" blocks of ⅝" plywood
(B) Four 24" by 36" panels of ¼" veneer
(C) Four 1 by 3s, 36"
(D) Four 1 by 3s, 22½"

Glue and nail together the 1 by 3s and ⅝" plywood for the box frames; don't add the veneer panels yet.

Now is the time to do any sanding and to finish the various wooden pieces with a couple of coats of clear polyurethane.

Next, make the cushions. Slightly sand one end of the dowels; then push them lengthwise through three of the foam cylinders. Cut them to 30". Through the fourth cylinder, push the spring.

Some foam dealers stock cylinders with holes through their centers. These are the best kind to buy for this project. If you can't find them, slice each cylinder lengthwise, using a serrated bread knife or an electric carving knife. Lay its dowel or spring in place along the center and rejoin the halves, using a foam adhesive. Wrap each bolster once around with batting and encase it in drawstring-style covers, discussed on page 80.

Mark placements for the dowels and spring on the two side panels,

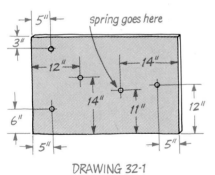

DRAWING 32-1

according to drawing 32-1. Drill ¼" holes at those marks. Then drill 3/16" pilot holes into the dowel ends, centered. Put washers onto the lag bolts, get your wrench ready, and, holding one of the bolsters in place, drive a lag through the plywood's hole and part way into the dowel's end. Repeat at the other

end and with the other dowels. A dowel, without a foam roll, belongs at the lower, back holes.

For the spring-held bolster, poke the eyebolts through the holes, add washers, and start the nuts onto the bolts. Hook on the spring; then tighten the nuts.

Check the chair to make sure it supports you comfortably. At this stage, you can change cylinder positions if necessary, drilling additional holes and rebolting them.

When you've established your proper seat contour, glue the 3" by 6" blocks to the outside of each hole (see drawing 32-2) and drill through

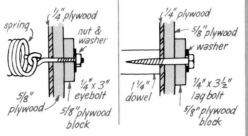

DRAWING 32-2

them. Glue and brad the inside panels (B) onto the plywood and drill through the holes again, this time piercing the veneer.

Next, glue and brad the outer panels onto the 1 by 3 frames. Add the oak threshold molding around the frame's perimeter, mitering the corners at 45° and gluing and brading them in place. Add rubber leg tips to bottom corners.

Set all brads below the surface. To enhance the chair's appearance, you can fill the brad holes and any gaps and then apply another coat of finish to those areas.

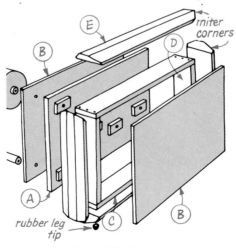

DRAWING 32-3

# Muffler-pipe chair

*This bold chair offers stylish lines and luxurious comfort.*

(Photo on page 31)

## Bare minimum tools:

Pencil
Measuring tape
Square
Compass
Power drill or drill press
Bits: expansive, ¼"
C-clamps
Table saw
Adjustable wrench
Sandpaper and finishing tools
Sewing equipment
Serrated bread knife

## Helpful tools:

Radial-arm saw
Jointer
Router
Band saw
Drill press
Power sander
Sewing machine
Electric carving knife

## Materials to buy:

(A) 16' of 1¾" o.d. muffler tubing
(B, C, D) 21' of 1⅜" by 3½" ash*
14 carriage bolts, ¼" by 3"
14 washers and cap nuts, ¼"
2 dowels, ¼" by 36"
6 yards of 36" wide canvas
Matching thread
2' by 4' of 4" foam
7 yards of 36" wide batting
White glue
Clear polyurethane finish

*Though ash was used for this chair, you could pick other hardwoods or even a strong softwood, such as Douglas fir.

## HERE'S HOW:

Begin with the tubing frame. Get prices from a few muffler shops for buying, cutting, and bending the tubing. Show drawing 33-1 to the attendant. Ask him to be as accurate

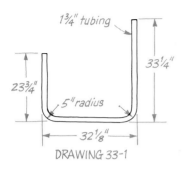

DRAWING 33-1

as possible: the bends should be a true 90°; the lengths should be carefully measured; and, when laid flat on the floor, the U shapes shouldn't rock. Before bending the tubing, look for a seam on the tubing and face it inward where it will be least visible.

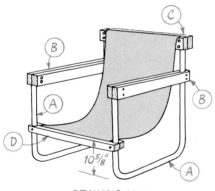

DRAWING 33-2

Cut the ash pieces to size. The wooden pieces (B,C,D) are each made up of two lengths fastened together. Pair these and clamp them together before cutting — but first rip the two pieces for (D) from one piece of ash. Mark each pair with a square. Cut the (B) pairs to 33⅛", the (C & D) pairs to 29⅝".

Leaving the clamps on the pairs, mark them for drilling 1¾" holes according to drawing 33-3. Because the 1¾" holes at the backside of each arm (B) and the front support (D) will go all the way through, mark "through" next to them. Mark 2¾" next to the front hole placements and the underside of (C); that's how deep to drill them.

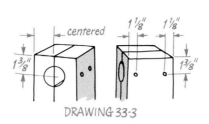

DRAWING 33-3

Hole diameters should match precisely the tubing diameter. Insure tight fit by using an expansive bit; test its size by drilling a hole and pushing the tubing through it.

Drill straight. (See more about drilling straight and cleanly on page 71.)

Keeping the pieces clamped together, mark for all ¼" bolt holes (see drawing 33-3). Drill them straight. Now unclamp the pairs, first marking them so they don't get mixed up.

Clamp one of the arm pairs (B) in place on one of the tubing sides (A), according to drawing 33-2. Double check the arm's level up from the floor; then use the holes in (B) as guides for drilling through the tubing. Be sure to drill straight so the bit will exit out the hole on the other side of (B). Put a bolt into each hole as you drill it. Add washers and nuts and snug them down.

Repeat for the other side. Then temporarily clamp the front support (D) to the front. Hold the back support (C) in place, drill holes, and add bolts. Then, after double checking your measurements, drill and bolt (D) in place.

Now is the time to treat the tubing to protect it from rusting. Remove the wood supports and arms. You can steel-wool the metal to a luster and follow with a couple of coats of polyurethane (which may slightly dull it). Or you can have it bright nickel plated by a metal plating company. To plate it should cost about $50.

Sand the wooden pieces, slightly beveling all of the pairs' outside edges and corners. Apply two coats of a clear polyurethane finish.

Replace the paired pieces, first spreading glue onto the inner faces of the arms (B). Bolt them in place and clamp the arms across their centers (protect the wood from clamp dents by slipping scrap wood under clamps' jaws). Don't glue any of the other pairs.

Next, make the sling. Cut a 61" length of canvas and fold under each long edge 3". Fold them again, this time 3¼". Pin and sew along both folds, ½" and 3" in from the edge.

Make the casings at the end of the sling as described on page 78. Cut the ¼" dowels to fit these casings.

Clamp the finished sling in place between the front support (D) and back support (C). Notice that the thickness of the fabric will not allow the two wooden halves to close completely. For full closure, you'll have to remove the wood where the fabric goes, using a router, table saw, or band saw.

Now make the cushions as shown in drawing 33-4. Cut the foam, using

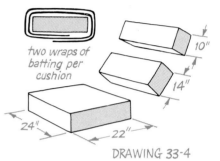

DRAWING 33-4

a bread knife or electric carving knife (see more about working with foam on page 78).

The cushion covers are the knife-edge style discussed on page 79, except that the corners are curved at a 1½" radius.

Make the two 3-inch-wide straps that hold the top cushion, allowing enough fabric for finishing the edges. Fold under 15" to make the loop. Stitch securely, backstitching at the beginning and end of each stitch.

After putting the cushions in place, arrange the head cushion's loops and sew them to the sling, as shown in drawing 33-5.

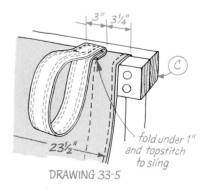

DRAWING 33-5

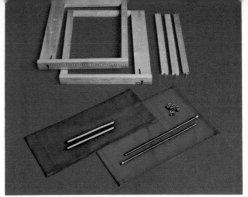

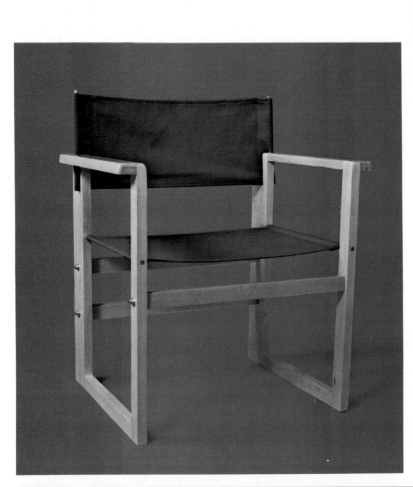

## Casual armchair
*See facing page*
*Design: Don Vandervort*

## Cheerful breakfast chair
*See page 37*
*Design: Don Vandervort*

# TAKE-APART CHAIRS OF CANVAS & BIRCH

Capturing the wind for schooners and providing a base for artistic masterpieces are two traditional uses of canvas. But canvas also has great possibilities for seating. Woven seat canvas — "chair duck" — follows body contours for comfort. It's washable, durable, and strong, and comes in a parade of colors and patterns.

These two chairs have canvas seats and birch frames. Birch was chosen here for its hardness and light coloring, but other similar hardwoods would work fine. In fact, you could make the blue chair from a strong softwood like Douglas fir (the chair gains strength through interlocking joinery and was designed to be made from softwood sizes).

Looser back support, comfortable arms, and lower seat height give the blue chair "easy chair" comfort. The orange chair offers comfortable desk or table-height seating. (The top of the orange chair's back may uncomfortably wedge the shoulders of a broad-shouldered person. To eliminate this problem, you can saw the front edge of the chair's back parallel with the angle of the canvas back.)

Construction is fairly basic. Doweling the side frame joints and cutting the long slots for canvas are the only techniques requiring a little know-how. If you plan to make several of these chairs, simplify your project by doing all the work for each step — such as cutting the leg lengths — at the same time.

For storage or moving, both chairs can be disassembled quickly into flat pieces by removal of a few screws or nuts.

## Casual armchair

*Comfortable sling seating makes this armchair ideal for desk work, conversation, or just relaxing.*

(Photo on facing page)

**Bare minimum tools:**

Pencil
Measuring tape
Square
Drill
Bits: ¼", ⅜", ½"
Handsaw*
Hacksaw**
Hammer or mallet
Adjustable wrench
Clamps
File (flat)
Sandpaper and finishing tools
Sewing equipment

*Pieces must be ripped to proper width or purchased as specified.

**Do without a hacksaw by having the metal rods cut to length.

**Helpful tools:**

Radial-arm saw
Coping saw or saber saw
Router, ¼" quarter-round and ¼" straight bits
Power sander
Sewing machine

**Materials to buy:**

(A,B,C) 12' of 1 by 2 birch
(D) 3½' of 1 by 3 birch
(E) 4¼' of 1 by 4 birch

*(Continued on next page)*

. . . Continued from page 35

(F,G) 4' of ⅜" doweling
(H,I) 5' of ⅜" round steel bar
6 hanger bolts, ¼" by 2½"
6 washers and cap nuts, ¼"
1 yard 30" wide canvas
Matching polyester thread
Wood filler
White glue
Clear polyurethane finish

## HERE'S HOW:

Begin by cutting (or having the lumberyard cut) the various pieces according to the cutting list below. If you use softwood, you must remove rounded edges where the legs (A,E) notch into the arms (D). Either you can rip one entire edge off (A) and (E) to remove the rounded portion or you can notch out a ¾" portion of the rounded edge as shown in drawing 36-1.

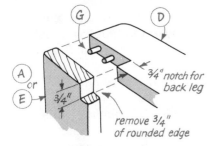

DRAWING 36-1

If you rip the edges, do it *before* cutting the pieces to length. If you notch the edges, do it *after* you cut the lengths. Mark and check all cuts using a square.

(A) Two ¾" by 1½", 25"
(B) Three ¾" by 1½", 20½"
(C) Two ¾" by 1½", 14½"
(D) Two ¾" by 2½", 19½"
(E) Two ¾" by 3½", 25"
(F) Eight ⅜" dowels, 3"
(G) Eight ⅜" dowels, 1½"

Front and back legs (A,E) notch into the arms (D) as shown in drawing 36-1. Mark for these notches, using each leg as a measure. Carefully cut the notches, using a coping saw, handsaw, or saber saw. Keep the blade perpendicular to the surfaces so the cuts don't run beyond the limiting lines.

On a flat surface, lay out the four pieces for each side frame the way they will be joined. Square the corners and snugly push together all pieces, keeping all surfaces flush. Mark straight lines for two dowels per corner; the 1½" dowels (G) at the arms and the 3" dowels (F) at

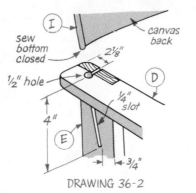

DRAWING 36-2

the bottom corners. Drill, glue, and dowel them together as explained on page 74.

Mark the slots in the 1 by 4s (E) according to drawing 36-2 and cut them, using any straight-cutting saw. Because this slot should be ¼" wide, you'll probably have to saw a couple of kerfs. After you glue the four frame pieces together, drill the ½" hole through the arm that connects with the slot.

Three crossbars (B) couple the two side frames. As shown in the detail (drawing 36-3), hanger bolts, screwed into the ends of the

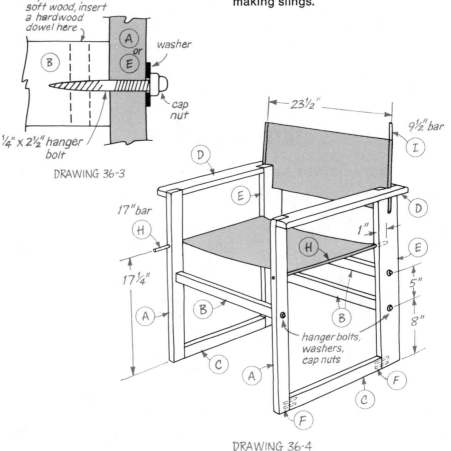

DRAWING 36-3

DRAWING 36-4

crossbars, poke through holes drilled in the side frames (A) and (E) and are tightened with washers and cap nuts. Drill the holes in the side frames as specified. The front crossbar (B) is 13" up from the floor.

Then screw the hanger bolts into the end grain of the crossbars. Do this by drilling a lead hole, running two nuts tightly together on the hanger bolt, and driving the top nut with a wrench. Remove the nuts when about 1" of the bolt protrudes.

Rout, file, or sand edges around top of arms to round them. Fill any gaps or mistakes, then sand the frames until smooth and even. Join the two completed frames with the crossbars.

Measure 17¼" up from the floor and mark the holes that hold the seat-sling bars (H). Drill these all the way through the front edge of (A) and about 1" into (E). If you don't want the metal of these bars to show from the front, cut them off ¾" shorter than specified and contact-cement a short (¾") length of dowel onto the front end of each.

Apply two coats of clear polyurethane finish. Last, make the slings with casings for the steel rods. See page 77 for information on making slings.

# Cheerful breakfast chair

*Brighten up your breakfast room with two or more of these stylish, comfortable chairs.*

(Photo on page 34)

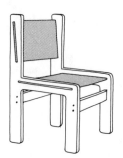

**Bare minimum tools:**

Pencil
Measuring tape
Compass
Square
Drill
Bits: #8 by 2" pilot, ¼", ⅜", ¾"
Coping saw
File (flat)
Bar or pipe clamps
Sewing equipment
Sandpaper and finishing tools

**Helpful tools:**

Radial-arm saw
Router, ¼" quarter-round and ¼"
 straight bits
Power sander
Sewing machine

**Materials to buy:**

(A,B,C,D) 15' of ¾" by 3½"
 birch
(E,F,G) 6' of ½" hardwood doweling
(H) 2' of ⅜" doweling
8 Phillips screws, 2" by #8
8 cup washers for screws
White glue
Wax (optional)
Wood filler
1 yard of 30" wide canvas
Matching polyester thread
Clear polyurethane finish

**HERE'S HOW:**

Cut all wood to length according to the following cutting schedule. Mark and check all cuts with a square. If you don't have the proper cutting tools, have the cuts made at the lumberyard.

(A) Two ¾" by 3½" birch, 32½"
(B) Two ¾" by 3½" birch, 19"
(C) Two ¾" by 3½" birch, 12½"
(D) Two ¾" by 3½" birch, 17½"
(E) Two ½" dowels, 15½"
(F) Two ½" dowels, 10"
(G) Four ¼" dowels, 3"
(H) Eight ⅜" dowels, 3"

Join the side pieces (A,B,C) as shown in the drawing, using dowels or splines (see page 74).

Next, cut the slots for the canvas. If you have a radial-arm saw, the easiest way is to line up a slot's marks beneath the saw's blade, clamp down the chair side, and slowly lower the blade into the wood.

An alternative way is to cut the slots with a router, clamping down the chair sides and making several shallow passes along a straight guide.

Or you can cut the slots using a saber saw, keyhole saw, or coping saw after first drilling a ¼" hole at each end. No matter how you cut them, be sure to file or sand the slots smooth.

Draw a radius for the rounded corners of (A) and (B) and cut them with a curve-cutting saw. Also cut the back angle if you plan to

modify the back (A) for a broad-shouldered person as previously mentioned. Then round the chair's exterior edges. If you have a router, this is easy — just put in a ¼" quarter-round bit and round all edges. Otherwise, you can sand them.

Strengthen (D) for holding screws by inserting a 3" by ¼" dowel (G) in a 3-inch-deep hole drilled in the underside, 1" from each end.

Mark the screw holes for mounting the cross pieces (D). Then, while holding the cross pieces in place, drill the screw pilot holes, counter-sinking them about ¼" deep and ¾" in diameter with a ¾" bit.

Wax the screws, push them through countersinking washers, and screw them in place. Fill any gaps or mistakes. Sand the entire chair frame and finish it with a clear polyurethane finish.

Finally, make the canvas slings with casings along the two narrow edges of each. Push the casings through the chair's slots and lock the slings in place with the ⅜" dowels. See page 77 for information on making slings.

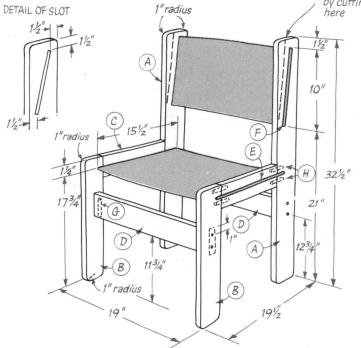

# STRAIGHT ONES: PLYWOOD, STACKABLE

Though most straight chairs require complex joinery and difficult woodworking techniques, some don't. Here are two chairs that require only a minimum of effort and expertise. If you can cut a straight line, you should be able to make them quite easily.

**The stackable chairs** are ideal where space is limited. When not in use, they stack piggyback. Their frames are mostly from 1 by 4s; fabric and foam on plywood form the seats and backs. Frame pieces are just glued and screwed together — you can paint or stain them, or finish them naturally. Those shown were given a red stain and a clear protective finish.

If you need several chairs, **plywood chairs** are a stylish, inexpensive answer. You can cut out material for six of them from two sheets of plywood. Choose a quality plywood like birch if you want to finish them naturally. If you plan to paint them, use standard plywood or, for very smooth surfaces, try density-overlaid plywood.

## Contemporary plywood chair

*You can cut six of these from two sheets of plywood.*

(Photo on facing page)

**Bare minimum tools:**

Pencil
Measuring tape
Square
Compass
Straightedge
Handsaw
Keyhole saw
Drill
Bits: ¼", 5/16", ¾", #10 by 1¼" pilot
Screwdriver
Sandpaper and finishing tools
Sewing equipment

**Helpful tools:**

Saber saw
Power circular saw
Table saw
Power sander
Sewing machine

**Materials to buy:**
(for three chairs)

1 sheet ¾" A-A birch plywood
18 slot-head bolts, ¼" by 1½"
24 slot-head bolts, ¼" by 3"
36 flathead screws, 1¼" by #10
42 T-nuts, ¼"
13' of ⅜" doweling
2⅔ yards of 30" wide canvas
White glue
Wood filler
Clear polyurethane finish

**HERE'S HOW:**

Begin by ripping the plywood sheet lengthwise along the two dimensions specified in drawing 40-1. If you don't have a table saw, it's best to have these cuts made at the lumberyard.

Next, draw on the plywood one each of the various pieces, measuring them according to drawings 40-2, 41-1, and 41-2. Cut out the side (A) piece, using a saber saw or keyhole saw inserted into ¾" holes where specified (finish long, straight cuts using a handsaw if you cut the curves with a keyhole saw).

Check the measurements for accuracy, sand any irregularities along the cut edges, and round all outside corners at a ⅜" radius. Use that finished side (A) as a template for laying out the remaining sides. Cut out all using same methods.

*(Continued on page 40)*

## Contemporary plywood chair

*See facing page*

*Design: Don Vandervort*

## Chairs for stacking

*See page 40*

*Design: Don Vandervort*

. . . Continued from page 38

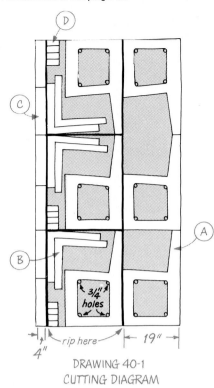

Cut one (B) piece roughly to size from a right-angle corner piece of the remaining section of plywood. Mark placement for (B) on the inside of (A); then use (A) as a template to transfer marks for the exact seat-angle and back-angle cuts (see drawing 40-2). Cut out (B) to finished size, curving the corners at a ⅜" radius. Mark that (B) piece to go with that (A) side.

Using the same methods, cut out the remaining (B) pieces and mark them to fit their corresponding side panels so they won't get mixed up.

Next, mark placement of the seven ¼" holes on one side panel (A) according to drawings 40-2 and 41-1. Drill the holes, backing each with scrap wood as you drill so the bit won't break away the plywood's backside. When all holes are drilled through that side panel, use it as a template for drilling the other sides.

Then align each (B) piece on its corresponding side panel (A) and use (A) as a drilling template again

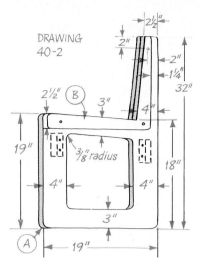

DRAWING 40-2

to drill through (B). Put a bolt in the first drilled hole; then drill the other two. Repeat with all other pairs.

Next, cut out, glue, and screw all 2¼" by 4" plywood blocks (D) to the horizontal supports (C). Each block (D) will bolt to a side (A) with two 3" bolts. You've already drilled the

---

# Chairs for stacking

*Piggyback chairs are made mostly from softwood 1 by 4s.*

(Photo on page 39)

## Bare minimum tools:

Pencil
Measuring tape
Square
Handsaw
Drill
Bits: #10 by 1¼", #8 by 2", #8 by ¾" pilots; ⅜"
⅜" plug-cutting bit
Screwdriver
Hammer or staple gun
Scissors
Sandpaper and finishing tools

## Helpful tools:

C-clamps
Table saw

Radial-arm saw
Power sander

## Materials to buy for one chair:

15' of 1 by 4 Clear pine
¼ sheet of ¾" A-D plywood
1' of 2 by 2 fir or pine
3' of ¼" doweling
12 screws, 1¼" by #10
20 screws, 2" by #8
8 screws, ¾" by #8
4 small angle brackets
2 foam slabs, 1" by 18" by 18"
1 yard 30" wide fabric
Staples or flat-head upholstery tacks
White glue
Wood filler
Colored stain
Polyurethane gloss finish

## HERE'S HOW:

Begin by cutting the 1 by 4s to length as follows. If you use a power saw, cut the legs in pairs to avoid discrepancies in their lengths. Use a square to mark and check your cuts.

(A) Two 1 by 4s, 31 "
(B) Two 1 by 4s, 17"
(C) Two 1 by 4s, 16½ "
(D) Two 1 by 4s, 17½ "

Also cut the back angle along the edge of the legs (A).

Make the frame that holds the seat (see drawing 40-3). Though the frames on the chairs in the photograph have interlocking corner joints, butt joints — when glued and screwed — are plenty strong and much easier to make. Don't add the corner blocks yet.

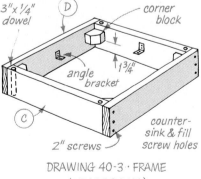

DRAWING 40-3 · FRAME
(UPSIDE DOWN)

Mark for the ¼" dowels in the undersides of (C), drill holes for them, add glue, and pound them in, cutting them off flush. These dowels give the screws strong wood to grip.

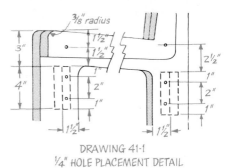

DRAWING 41-1
¼" HOLE PLACEMENT DETAIL

bolt holes through (A), so now you must duplicate them through the edge of (D).

Intersect the two bolt holes with one pencil line, extending it a couple of inches beyond the holes. Align this center line with the center of the edge of (D) and, holding (D) firmly in place, drill into it through the two holes in (A). Drill as deeply as the bit will go; then remove (D) and finish drilling through it. Carefully hammer T-nuts into (D) where specified, positioning the

teeth so they don't split the plywood.

Be sure the chair is standing on a flat, level surface when you drill and fasten the second side panel (A) of each chair to the other end of each horizontal support. Now you can assemble the chair with the proper bolts and T-nuts.

Fill all voids in the plywood with wood filler and add the finish.

Then make the seat and back slings to fit. The seat sling is held by dowels in a casing, on the underside of (B), and the back is held the same way at the backside of (B). The 1½" bolts poke through the canvas. See how to make slings on page 77.

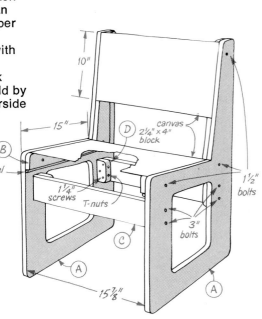

DRAWING 41-2
COMPLETED
ASSEMBLY

Then, hold or clamp the connecting (C) and (D) pieces squarely together, drill pilot holes, glue, and screw them.

Lay the frame upside down on a piece of ¾" plywood and mark the frame's inside perimeter on the plywood. For the seat base (E), cut to the *inside* of the lines (this creates an allowance for the fabric). Be sure the frame is square when you use it to mark the plywood.

Mark the frame's position on the legs (A,B), using a square. Then put the #10 by 1¼" pilot bit in the drill.

If you have C-clamps, secure the legs to the frame and make any necessary adjustments to level the chair. If you're not using C-clamps, get your drill handy and hold each leg securely as you drill. Be sure to drill the pilot holes from the *inside* of the frame. Don't drill through. Do this with each leg, gluing and screwing them from the inside.

Add corner blocks. Trim off their corners and recess them 1¾" below the frame's top edge. Glue and fasten them in place with a few nails or two screws each.

Next, cut the 7½" by 17½" plywood back from ¾" plywood and mark its placement on the legs (A).

Gather the cut fabric, foam, and

staple gun (or hammer and flat upholstery tacks). Wrap the back as shown in drawing 41-3, stretching the top down and fastening it along the plywood's side edges, keeping the fasteners as flat as possible.

Bevel corners, fill gaps and mistakes, sand, and add the colored stain and clear finish (or whatever finishes you'd like) to the wooden frame.

Putting the pilot bit for the 2" by #8 screws in the drill, mark placement of the screws that secure the back to (A). Firmly hold the back in place and carefully drill through (A) into the back's edges, counter-sinking about ¼" with a ⅜" bit. Drive in the screw for each hole as you drill.

Cut plugs from scrap wood for filling the countersunk screw holes in (A). Spread a little glue on their undersides, push them in place, and sand them flush with the wood's surface. Touch them up with stain and finish.

Next, cut the seat foam the same size as the plywood base. Lay it on the plywood, wrap the fabric around it, and staple or tack the fabric around the perimeter of the plywood's underside. Fasten the seat to the frame with small angle brackets.

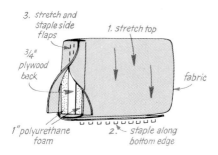

DRAWING 41-3

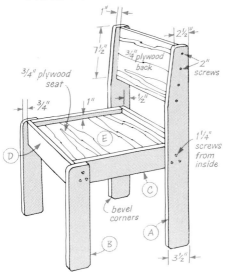

# Pine trestle table

*Design: Greg Smith,*
*The Just Plain Smith Co.*

*Adding the leaves*

*Trestle table as a desk*

# PINE TRESTLE TABLE

Embarrassment strikes your dinner guest. His face flushes burgundy, the same color as the wine he just spilled by accidentally knocking the table leg with his knees.

If this happens often, maybe you need a trestle table like this one. The strong trestle base eliminates those troublesome legs at the table's corners. (A pedestal base will solve that problem, too. See page 50.)

Featured on this book's front cover, the trestle table is made from inexpensive softwood. The #3 Common pine that was used gives the top its distinction through knots, streaks, and stains. And the table is relatively easy to make. The base is bolted together and the top boards glued and nailed to a plywood surface. Two removable leaves allow it to serve as a large dining table, a medium-size table, or a personal desk.

## Bare minimum tools:

Pencil
Measuring tape
Square
Handsaw
Hammer
Nailset (or large nail)
Screwdriver
Drill
Bits: #8 by 1½″ and #12 by 2½″
  pilots, ⅜″, 1″
C-clamps
Sandpaper and finishing tools

## Helpful tools:

Bar clamps
Doweling jig
Drill press
Power circular saw
Radial-arm saw
Power sander

## Materials to buy:

(A,B) 20′ of 2 by 4 pine
(C) 4′ of 2 by 6 pine
(D) 6′ of 2 by 3 Clear fir or pine
(E,I) 12′ of 2 by 2 Clear fir or pine
(F,G,H) 78′ of 1 by 4 #3 Common pine
(J) Scrap of ½″ plywood,
  1½′ square
(K) 4′ by 8′ sheet of ¾″ A-D plywood
15 table pins (dowel pegs), ⅜″ by
  1¼″
4 hex-head bolts, ⅜″ by 2½″
4 hex-head bolts, ⅜″ by 4″
4 hex-head bolts, ⅜″ by 8″ (or
  threaded rods)
12 hex nuts, ⅜″
24 flat washers, ⅜″
4 flathead screws, 2½″ by #12
16 flathead screws, 1½″ by #8
3 window catches with screws
¼ pound of 6d finish nails
White glue
Wood filler
Clear polyurethane sealer-finish
Flat black paint

## HERE'S HOW:

Start by marking and cutting most of the wood to size. (You'll find hints for accurate cutting on page 69.) Double check your measurements and use a square to mark the cutting lines.

Though all cutting measurements are given below, wait to cut the pieces labeled (G) until after you assemble the other 1 by 4s that make up the top.

## Cutting schedule:

(A) Four 2 by 4s, 30″
(B) Four 2 by 4s, 27″
(C) One 2 by 6, 40½″
(D) Two 2 by 3s, 30″
(E) Two 2 by 2s, 46¼″
(F) Two 1 by 4s, 72″
(G) Two 1 by 4s, 35″ (wait)
(H) Ten 1 by 4s, 71″
(I) Eight 2 by 2s, about 12″
(J) Four ½″ plywood, 4½″ by 4½″
(K) One ¾″ plywood, 35″ by 71″

*(Continued on next page)*

. . . Continued from page 43

Cut lower corners off the pieces labeled (D) as shown in drawing 44-5.

Then make the table top. Lay the plywood face up on a work surface, and lay the 1 by 4s (H) on top the way you want them.

Beginning at one side, spread white glue on the underside of the 1 by 4 and lay it in place, flush with the plywood along the edge and at both ends. Clamp down the 1 by 4 (protect wood from clamp's jaws by

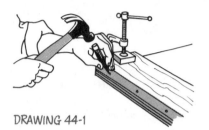

DRAWING 44-1

adding a scrap wood block). Blind nail the 1 by 4 to the plywood with 6d finish nails as shown in drawing 44-1. Using a square, mark where cuts for leaves will be and do not nail there.

Spread glue on the bottom and

adjoining edge of the next 1 by 4 and butt the glued edge against the first 1 by 4. Before nailing, use bar clamps (if you have them) to cinch it tightly against the first 1 by 4 (see drawing 44-2). Blind nail in the same fashion. Again, mark it for the saw

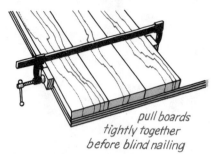

pull boards
tightly together
before blind nailing

DRAWING 44-2

cuts and don't nail there.

Continue this process for succeeding 1 by 4s across the rest of the surface.

When the glue dries, clamp down a straightedge to guide your saw directly across the lines designating the leaves (see drawings 44-3 and

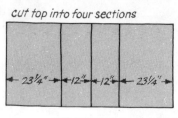

cut top into four sections

←23¼"→ ←12"→ ←12"→ ←23¼"→

DRAWING 44-3

44-4). Make these cuts as straight and uniform as you possibly can — any discrepancies will show up later as gaps. Notice the two scraps in drawing 44-4 that raise the

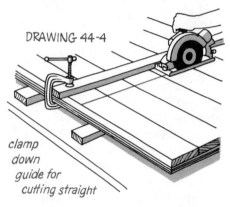

DRAWING 44-4

clamp
down
guide for
cutting straight

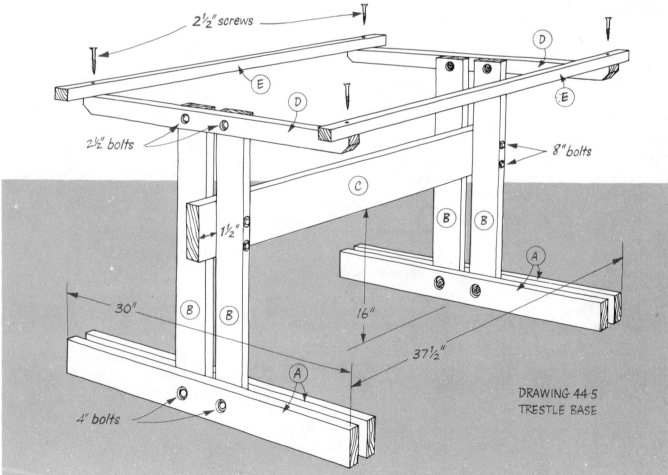

2½" screws

E

D

D

E

2½" bolts

8" bolts

C

B

B

1½"

B

B

A

30"

16"

37½"

A

A

4" bolts

DRAWING 44-5
TRESTLE BASE

surface up off the worktable so the circular saw blade won't cut the worktable.

Butt the top sections together and mark them for table pins as shown in drawing 45-1. Because the pins in all leaves must match perfectly, be sure your measurements are right on.

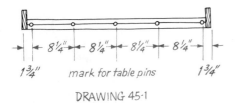

DRAWING 45-2

clamp pieces and drill bolt holes

DRAWING 45-3

8¼"  8¼"  8¼"  8¼"

1¾"  mark for table pins  1¾"

DRAWING 45-1

See page 74 for information on making dowel joints. Use the information regarding drilling straight and matching up the holes, but remember that you are not permanently joining the two edges. Since the table pins are used for aligning leaves as you slide the sections together, you glue them into only one of each pair of meeting edges.

Pound the 1¼" table pins into the holes in one side of each leaf and the table top until they protrude ¾". Use a block (see drawing 45-2) to stop them. If you use dowels instead of table pins, lightly sand the dowel tips so they insert easily into the matching holes.

Screw window catches to the

matching halves of the underside of the leaves. These catches should all be centered exactly 17½" from one edge of the table.

Finish the edges of the table top by cutting, gluing, and finish-nailing 1 by 4s around the perimeter. Countersink the nail heads and fill the holes.

Then make the trestle base. Join the pieces with C-clamps. Check everything for square. Mark (C) placement on the (B) pieces first. Then center and bolt the (B) pieces to the (A) and (D) pieces. Follow by attaching (C). Drill the 1" by ½" deep countersinking holes, then the ⅜" holes for bolts (see drawing 45-3).

Paint the bolt heads, washers, and nuts black. Screw the rails onto the top of the trestle and sand them so they will slide smoothly.

Turn the top upside down on your work surface (don't mar it) and set the trestle in place, upside down and centered. Mark the placement of the 2 by 2 rail guides (I); then glue and nail them in place. Allow for smooth rail movement. Screw the ½" plywood scrap (J) onto the rail guides — not onto the rail.

Set the table right side up and inspect it to make sure everything works properly. If the rails balk, try waxing them. Make any necessary adjustments; then sand the table carefully and apply clear polyurethane sealer-finish.

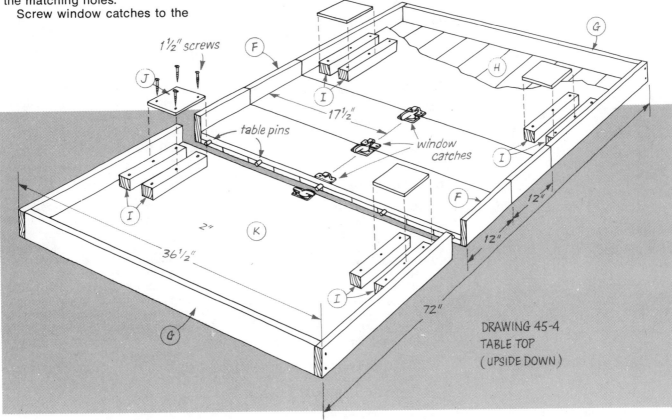

DRAWING 45-4
TABLE TOP
(UPSIDE DOWN)

# PARSONS TABLES

These three tables are not called "Parsons tables" because they were originally used by clergy. Instead, their name comes from the Parsons School of Design, where their distinctive style was developed. Though Parsons tables are presently enjoying a widespread popularity, they aren't new; they've been around since the 1930s.

A Parsons table complements many styles of furniture. Typically, such tables are cubical, but, as shown here, they can be built in several sizes to suit various needs. One of the table's primary traits is the relationship between its various dimensions. If you vary sizes, keep leg cross sections square and the same width as the top rails.

## Sleek dining table

*Elegant dining table seats six comfortably, eight in a pinch.*

(Photo on facing page)

**Bare minimum tools:**

Pencil
Measuring tape
Square
Handsaw
Drill
Bit: #10 by 2″ pilot
Hammer
Sandpaper and finishing tools

**Helpful tools:**

Table saw with dado blade
Radial-arm saw
Power sander
Power sprayer

**Materials to buy:**

(A) 10′ of 4 by 4*
(B,C) 19′ of 1 by 4*
(D,E,F,G) 24′ of 1 by 2*
(H) 4′ by 8′ sheet of ¾″ hardboard-
    veneered plywood
24 flathead screws, 2″ by #10
Small box 6d finishing nails
Small box 3d nails
Wood filler
White glue
Polyurethane finish (gloss black)

   *Because all pieces are filled and

painted, you don't have to buy expensive defect-free lumber. Just be sure lumber is sturdy and straight.

**HERE'S HOW:**

To provide a smooth, tough surface, hardboard-veneered plywood forms the top of this table. It is set in a frame of 1 by 4s and supported by hidden 1 by 2s. The frame and top stand on 4 by 4 legs.

Cut most of the pieces to size, according to the following cutting schedule (page 48). Cut the plywood top (H) first. Then check its size to be sure all the adjoining pieces will fit it. Don't necessarily cut all pieces at once; to insure tight fit, remeasure and cut pieces as you assemble. (See hints for cutting straight and cleanly on page 69.)

*(Continued on page 48)*

## Sleek dining table

*See facing page*

*Design adaptation:*
*Jim Mitchell*

## Bedside table

*See page 49*

*Design adaptation:*
*Jim Mitchell*

## Leather patchwork Parsons

*See page 49*

*Design adaptation: Rick Morrall*

*. . . Continued from page 46*

## Cutting schedule:

(A) Four 4 by 4s, 28¼"
(B) Two 1 by 4s, 66"
(C) Two 1 by 4s, 42½"
(D) Two 1 by 2s, 37"
(E) Two 1 by 2s, 42½"
(F) Two 1 by 2s, 21¼"
(G) Four 1 by 2s, 18⅛"
(H) One ¾" plywood, 42½" by 64½"

Lay out the notches in the tops of the legs (A), using a square or tape measure and straightedge (see drawing 48-1). Saw to the waste

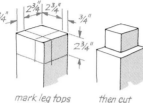

mark leg tops      then cut
DRAWING 48-1

side of the cutting lines, beginning with the cuts perpendicular to the wood grain and finishing with the cuts into the end grain.

After laying the plywood (H) face down on a flat surface, position the 1 by 4s (B,C) around it. To save on filling and sanding later, consider

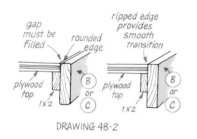

DRAWING 48-2

removing (ripping) one of the rounded edges from these 1 by 4s in a table saw or with a router (see drawing 48-2).

Check the corners to be sure they fit together flush and squarely. And be sure the table top's surface will be flush with the upper edge of those 1 by 4s, as in drawing 48-2. Then spread glue along the plywood edges, push the 1 by 4s in place, and nail them every 6" with 6d finishing nails, setting the heads below the surface.

When the glue dries, fit a 4 by 4 leg (A) into place at a corner and drill screw pilot holes, countersinking them. Before drilling, be sure those legs are square and straight up and down. Spread glue on the adjoining surfaces (unless you want to make legs removable by only screwing them on). Then screw through the 1 by 4s (B,C) into the leg with 2" by #10 screws. Do this to all four legs. Also screw the center rails (E) in place as shown in drawing 48-3,

countersinking the heads.

Add the 1 by 2s (D,F,G) — as shown — with glue and 3d nails. Let the glue dry; then fill all holes and gaps, sand until smooth (avoid sanding the hardboard), and apply two or three coats of polyurethane.

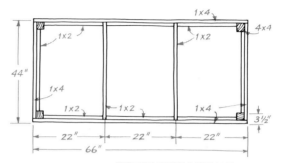

TOP VIEW OF TABLE FRAMING

DRAWING 48-3

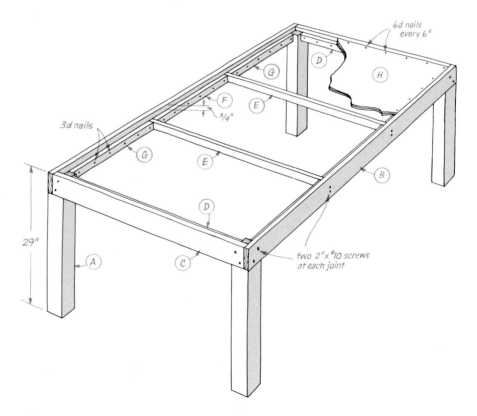

# Bedside table

*Here is a versatile size that's handy anywhere.*

(Photo on page 47)

**Bare minimum tools:**

Pencil
Measuring tape
Square
Handsaw
Drill
Bit: #10 by 2" pilot
Hammer
Sandpaper and finishing tools

**Helpful tools:**

Router
Table saw
Power sander

**Materials to buy:**

¼ sheet of ¾" hardboard-veneered
  plywood
7' of 4 by 4
8' of 1 by 4
6' of 1 by 2
16 flathead screws, 2" by #10
Small box of 6d nails
Small box of 3d nails
Wood filler
White glue
Paint or finish

**HERE'S HOW:**

Except for being smaller, this table is made just like the larger dining table that precedes it. The directions for making it are virtually the same; only the dimensions differ. Use the following cutting schedule and the drawings on the facing page for building it. Make one structural revision: don't fasten center rails (E) beneath the top — small tables don't need this added support.

(A) Four 4 by 4s, 21"
(B) Two 1 by 4s, 23"
(C) Two 1 by 4s, 21½"
(D) Two 1 by 2s, 16"
(G) Two 1 by 2s, 16"
(H) One ¾" plywood, 21½" by 21½"

# Leather patchwork Parsons

*Patches of leather tacked to this table give it a rich, handcrafted look.*

(Photo on page 47)

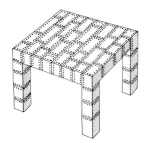

The following directions are for covering a 24-inch-square Parsons table with leather scraps. To make the table, see the preceding directions for the Parsons bedside table and modify the dimensions.

**Bare minimum tools:**

Scissors
Tack hammer
Shoeshine brush

**Materials to buy:**

About 1½ pounds of leather scraps
1 pound of mixed #4 and #8
  upholstery tacks
Dark color of leather dye (mahogany)
Shoe polish (oxblood)
Colorless, water-repellent leather
  dressing

**Material notes:**

Buy leather scraps from a leather shop. Pick the biggest pieces and greatest variety of color and texture available, but don't choose soft suedes or chamois — they'll stretch out of shape. When pieces are dyed, different colored leathers show only subtle differences in color.

Saddle, shoe repair, and leather shops sell several types of water-repellent leather dressings.

**HERE'S HOW:**

To start, cut out a leather rectangle and position it, smooth side up, anywhere on the table. Stretch it slightly but don't distort it too much. Push in tacks ¼" to 1" apart along the edges.

When the tacks are in place, give each a light tap with a tack hammer so it won't bounce out while you pound in the others. Drive each tack in all the way; then continue to cut and tack. Butt the pieces up tightly to each other, varying the size, shape, texture, and color as you go. Pieces can end at corners or wrap around them, as you like.

Banging tacks is noisy work. To partially deaden the drum, you can prop a piece of wood between the floor and table center as a fifth leg to keep the table from jumping under the hammer blows.

When the table is completely covered, paint it with full-strength, dark-colored leather dye. Though the table may look very dark at first, it should lighten in about a week.

When the dye is dry, heavily coat the leather with shoe polish, using the applicator brush. Rub the polish into the cracks between leather pieces. When the polish dries, buff the table to a gloss with a shoeshine brush. Finally, coat the table with a colorless, water-repellent leather dressing to seal it and help protect against water marks and soiling.

## Rectangular oak table

*See facing page*
*Design: Jim Mitchell*

## Circular pedestal table

*See page 52*
*Design: Frank Bletsch*

# PEDESTAL TABLES

Unlike small, corner-legged tables that corral your knees, forcing you to "scoot" under them rather than "sit down" to them, pedestal tables give you leg room. Because a pedestal table doesn't have corner legs, it gives you room to maneuver. In addition, the usually round, square, or almost square shape of pedestal tables tends to focus dinner activity and conversation.

Two pedestal tables are discussed here: one is rectangular, the other is round. **The rectangular table's** top is made from oak boards laminated onto plywood. Its pedestal is a simply made hollow oak box.

**The circular table** has a solid wood top, formed by gluing together several boards. Though the one shown is made from hemlock, you could substitute pine or fir. The base is particularly easy to make.

# Rectangular oak table

*Just cut the boards square, apply glue,*
*and screw them together.*

(Photo on facing page)

**Bare minimum tools:**

Pencil
Measuring tape
Square
Saw
Drill
Bits: #8 by 1″, #8 by 2″, #12 by 2½″ pilots; plug cutter; ¼″
Screwdriver
Sandpaper and finishing tools

**Helpful tools:**

Miter box
Clamps
Radial-arm saw
Table saw
Drill press
Power sander

**Materials to buy:**

(A,B,C) 60′ of ¾″ by 3½″ oak
(D) 4′ by 4′ sheet of ¾″ plywood
(E) 10′ of ¾″ by 8½″ oak
(F) 8′ of ¾″ by 5½″ oak
(G) 3′ of 2 by 2 fir
22 flathead screws, 1″ by #8
36 flathead screws, 2″ by #8
8 flathead screws, 2½″ by #12
8 carriage bolts, ¼″ by 2½″
8 washers and nuts, ¼″
Aliphatic resin or urea resin glue
Wood filler
Clear polyurethane finish

**HERE'S HOW:**

Cutting comes first. Be sure to use a square to mark and check all cuts. Refer to drawing 52-1 (next page).

Begin by cutting the 11 top surface pieces (A) to 46½″. If you own a power saw, cut them slightly oversize and trim all ends off at once after gluing and screwing them to the plywood base. Cut the plywood base (D) to 38½″ by 46½″.

Align one (A) piece along one of the plywood's long edges, flush at both ends. Firmly hold or clamp it in place and drill the 1″ by #8 screw pilot holes 7¾″ from each end, countersinking ¼″ for wooden plugs. Spread glue along the board's (A) underside, hold or clamp it in place, and drive in the screws.

Repeat this process, butting the next (A) piece firmly against the secured one. If you have clamps, use

*(Continued on next page)*

... Continued from page 51

them to pull it up tight. Spread glue along the joining edges. If you won't be trimming off the ends with a power saw, be sure to keep them all perfectly flush.

Frame the finished top with ¾" by 3½" oak (B) and (C). This table's frame corners were mitered, glued, and clamped with pipe clamps. If you don't have a miter box or clamps, you can butt join the pieces, glue, and screw them (plugging the screw holes). Use the finished top for measuring the proper lengths of frame pieces.

The pedestal is simply a box. Cut the four pieces (E) to 27". Mark for the screw pilot holes, holding or clamping the pieces together. Apply glue and fasten with 2" screws. Be sure ends are flush.

Add feet (F) to the pedestal. Cut the 5½" oak to four 22" lengths. Glue and screw them around the pedestal's base as shown in drawing 53-1, keeping the pedestal vertical. Next, using the plug cutter, cut plugs

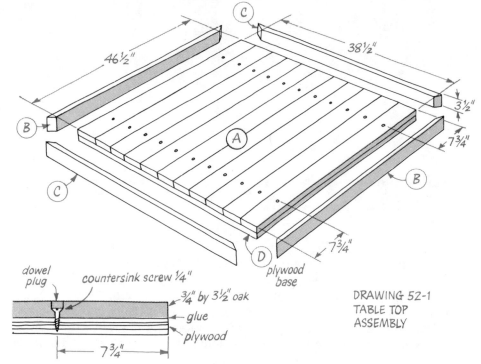

DRAWING 52-1
TABLE TOP
ASSEMBLY

# Circular pedestal table

*Butcher block-style top and bolt-together base combine to form this good-looking, sturdy pedestal table.*

(Photo on page 50)

## Bare minimum tools:

Pencil
Measuring tape
Square
Compass
Yardstick
Saber saw
Handsaw
Drill
Bits: 3/16", 5/16", ⅜"
Pipe or bar clamps
Adjustable wrench
Pliers or another wrench
Sandpaper and finishing tools

## Helpful tools:

Table saw
Jointer
Drill press
Doweling jig
Power sander

## Materials to buy:

(A,B) 42' of 2 by 6
(C,D) 16' of 2 by 3
Doweling or splines for top
2 hex-head machine bolts, ⅜" by 7"
2 hex-head machine bolts, ⅜" by 5"
4 hex-head machine bolts, 5/16" by 7"
2 hex-head machine bolts, 5/16" by 5"
8 lag bolts, 5/16" by 3½" with washers
1 nut and 2 washers for each of the machine bolts (use 1" outside-diameter washers for the ⅜" bolts)
Aliphatic resin or urea resin glue
Clear polyurethane finish

## HERE'S HOW:

Begin by cutting the lumber to length. Here's what you'll need:

(A) Nine 2 by 6s, 48"
(B) Two 2 by 6s, 32"
(C) Four 2 by 3s, 28½"
(D) Two 2 by 3s, 32"

Softwood boards have rounded edges. The boards that form the top (A) must have their rounded edges removed before they can be joined. Run them through a table saw or jointer to do this. If you don't have the proper tools, take the boards to a cabinetmaker or planing mill.

Refer to the how-to section, page 75, for information on making glued-up tops. Mark circle on top, cut with saber saw, and sand edge.

Making the base is easy. Begin by marking the centers of the (B) and (D) pieces and cutting interlocking notches as shown in drawing 53-2.

from oak scraps for all countersunk holes. Glue them in place and sand them off flush.

Cut the 2 by 2 to four 8½" lengths. Hold these blocks flush with the pedestal's top edges, drill ¼" bolt holes, add glue, and bolt the blocks in place, using two 2½" bolts per block.

Turn the table top and pedestal upside down. Center the pedestal on the top's underside. Drill pilot holes and screw the blocks to the top, using two 2½" screws per block. By not applying glue, you'll be able to remove the top.

Fill any gaps, sand all surfaces, and apply two coats of polyurethane.

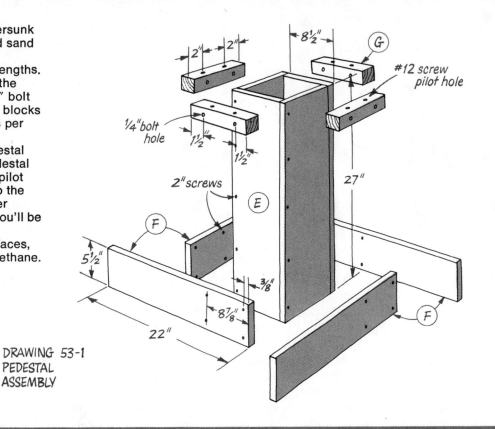

DRAWING 53-1
PEDESTAL
ASSEMBLY

Next, mark the uprights (C) for drilling the holes, according to drawing 53-3. Drill all holes prior to assembly. By drilling them slightly

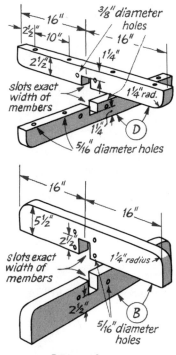

DRAWING 53-2

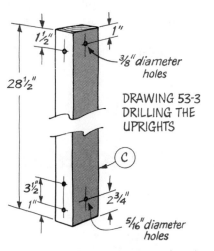

DRAWING 53-3
DRILLING THE
UPRIGHTS

oversized, you can ease putting the pieces together. Be sure to drill straight (see more about drilling on page 71).

Using the holes in the uprights (C) as patterns, drill holes in the sides of (B) and (D).

Assemble the pieces with bolts, washers, and nuts. Use ⅜" bolts for the upper assembly (C-D), 5/16" bolts for the lower assembly (B-C).

Drill 5/16" pilot holes through (D) for the lag bolts that hold the top in place. Turn the top upside down and center the pedestal on it, upside

down. Drill 3/16" holes 1" into the top where the lag bolts go, slide a washer onto each lag, and drive lags through (D) into the holes.

Sand all surfaces and finish with at least two coats of polyurethane.

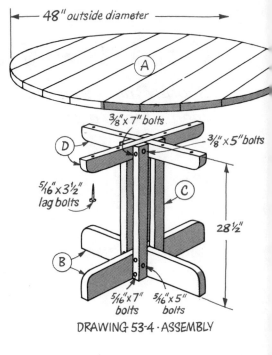

DRAWING 53-4 · ASSEMBLY

# HANDY, FOLD-UP PLYWOOD TABLES

Extra tables are very convenient for activities other than eating. But many rooms are just not large enough to hold more than one table.

For use where you don't need a permanent table, here are three hard-working fold-up tables. One is a flat-folding game table; another is a fold-against-the-wall table; the third is a worktable on collapsible sawhorses.

Relatively inexpensive, all three are made primarily from birch plywood. (Density-overlaid plywood would provide a smooth, paintable, less-expensive surface.) All are reasonably easy to make (a saber saw helps, but that's as sophisticated a tool as you'll need).

**The sawhorse craft table's** size is variable. The top and shelf shown are what you get when the lumberyard attendant rips a plywood sheet 32″ from one edge. You can adjust the table's height simply by changing the spread of the sawhorse base.

Use **the wall table** for practically any purpose: desk, dining table, or even a changing table in a baby's room. When it's folded up, you can disguise it with a bulletin board, dartboard, wall hanging, or anything you'd ordinarily hang on the wall. Or you can leave it exposed.

Four can play at **the round game table** — but no more. For a larger group, make a larger top. From a half sheet of plywood, you can cut a 4-foot-diameter top. Fasten it to the base using the same methods described.

# Fold-to-wall worktable

*Slightly more than half a sheet of plywood makes this roomy table/desk.*

(Photo on facing page)

**Bare minimum tools:**
Pencil
Measuring tape
Straightedge
Handsaw
Hacksaw
File
Screwdriver
Drill
Bit: 3/16″
Sandpaper and finishing tools

**Helpful tools:**
Compass
Saber saw
Table saw
Power sander

**Materials to buy:**
4′ by 8′ sheet of ¾″ birch A-B plywood
1 continuous hinge, 1″ by 72″, with screws
1 cork bulletin board, 32″ by 40″ (optional)

*(Continued on page 56)*

## Fold-to-wall worktable

*See facing page*
*Design: Don Vandervort*

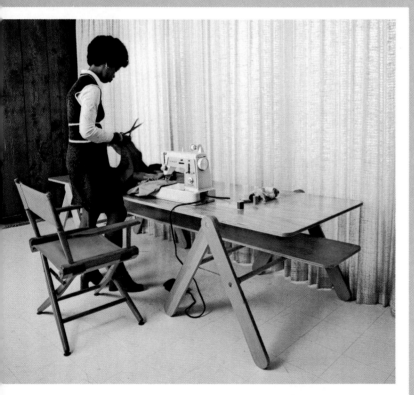

## Sawhorse craft table

*See page 56*
*Design: Don Vandervort*

## Round game table

*See page 56*
*Design: Donald Wm.*
*MacDonald, AIA*

. . . Continued from page 54

1 barrel bolt, 2½″
6 screws, 2″ (or toggle bolts) for
  wall mount
1 large gate hook and eyebolt
Clear polyurethane finish

### HERE'S HOW:

First cut out the top (A), leg (B),
wall-mounting piece (C), and barrel
bolt block (D) as shown in the cutting
diagram (drawing 56-1). If you have

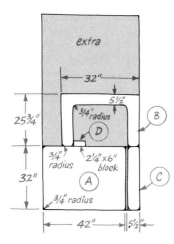

PLYWOOD CUTTING DIAGRAM
DRAWING 56-1

a saber saw or some other curve-
cutting saw, round the corners as
indicated. Otherwise, just cut them
square and sand them.

Sand the edges and lightly sand
the surfaces with 220-grit sandpaper
wrapped around a block.

Next, apply the first coat of clear
finish to all plywood and let it dry
thoroughly. When it's dry, sand it
lightly with 400-grit sandpaper. Then
apply a second coat of finish. For
an extremely smooth finish, repeat
the two-coat process.

Using a hacksaw, cut the hinge
into two 30″ lengths; file away any
burrs. Following drawing 56-2,
attach the hinge to the top (A) and

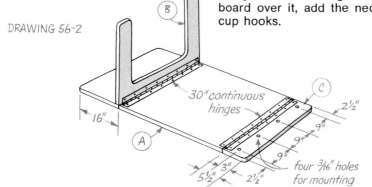

DRAWING 56-2

the wall mount (C), using flathead
screws. Attach the leg (B) to the
underside of the top (A) the same
way. Then drill the four 3/16″
holes through (C) as shown in
drawing 56-2.

To hold the leg (B) in place when
the table is down, screw in a gate
hook and eyebolt (drawing 56-3).

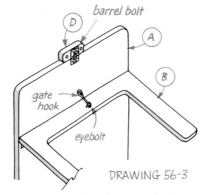

DRAWING 56-3

Approximate the placement of the
table. Mark the wall 25¾″ from the
floor twice, separating the marks
about 2′. Then have someone hold
the table in place so that the top
edge of (C) is flush with those marks.

Drill through the existing holes in
(C) and screw to wall studs or fasten
with toggle bolts.

Collapse the table against the wall
and mark for placement of the barrel
bolt block (D) on the wall directly
in line with the table top's (A) top
edge. Assemble the barrel bolt block

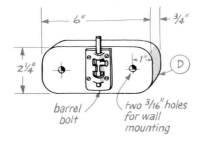

DRAWING 56-4  BARREL BOLT BLOCK

(D) as shown in drawing 56-4; then
drill pilot holes and attach.

If you want to hang a bulletin
board over it, add the necessary
cup hooks.

# Round game table

*Flatten it by revolving the
four braces and folding
down the legs.*

(Photo on page 55)

### Bare minimum tools:

Pencil
Measuring tape
Compass
Square
Yardstick
Saber saw
Screwdriver
Hammer
Hacksaw
Drill
Bit: ¼″ long shank
Sandpaper and finishing tools

### Helpful tools:

Table saw
Drill press
Power sander

# Sawhorse craft table

*Easy-to-make, generous
table stores in minimum
space.*

(Photo on page 55)

### Bare minimum tools:

Pencil
Measuring tape
Compass
Coping saw
Hammer or mallet

## Materials to buy:

1 sheet of ¾" birch A-A plywood
4 carriage bolts, ¼" by 5½"
4 carriage bolts, ¼" by 3"
12 flat washers, ¼"
8 lock washers and hex nuts, ¼"
8 butt hinges, 2"
4 rubber leg tips
Wood filler
Clear polyurethane finish

## HERE'S HOW:

Begin by duplicating the plywood layout (drawing 57-1) on your sheet of plywood. (Refer to the various drawings for measurements.) Use a yardstick, tacking one end to the center point, to guide drawing the circular top (A).

Using a saber saw, cut out the pieces (saw to the outside of the lines). After cutting out the four legs (B), mark and cut the center portion (C) from each leg. Hopefully, the saw kerf will create an allowance that's

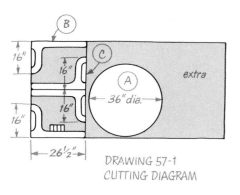

DRAWING 57-1
CUTTING DIAGRAM

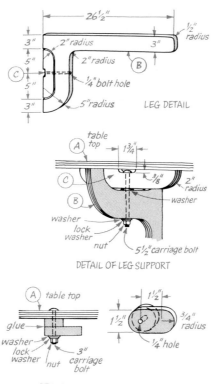

LEG DETAIL

DETAIL OF LEG SUPPORT

DRAWING 57-2 SWIVEL CATCH

the same thickness as the washer. This way, when you later insert the washer in the bolt, the level across the top of the leg will be straight. Sand all edges.

Next, drill the bolt holes. These must be perfectly straight. Of course, the best tool for this is a drill press. If you drill it improperly, pound a ¼" dowel into it, cut it off

flush, and try again. (See hints for drilling straight on page 71.)

Put the bolts in, hammer them down tight, and add the legs. Use a hacksaw to cut off the bolts flush.

Lay the legs in place and mark both the leg tops and the table underside for hinge screws. First screw the hinges to the legs and then to the table. Add rubber tips.

Cut out the swivel catch pieces and sand them until smooth and round. Drill ¼" holes as specified and bolt them in place. You can countersink the bolt heads if you want to.

Sand and fill any irregularities in the surface or the edges and add a clear finish.

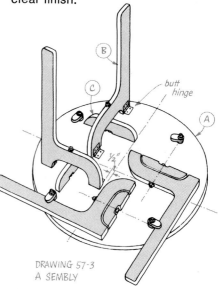

DRAWING 57-3
ASSEMBLY

---

Drill
Bits: expansive or 1" spade, ¼"
Sandpaper and finishing tools

## Helpful tools:

Saber saw
Drill press
Table saw

## Materials to buy:

4' by 8' sheet of birch A-B plywood
20' of 1 by 4 Clear pine or fir
6 hardwood dowels, 1" by 3'
1 dowel, ¼" by 3'
4 lengths of sash chain, 24" each
White glue
Clear polyurethane finish

## HERE'S HOW:

By having the plywood and 1 by 4s cut at the lumberyard, you won't

need straight-cutting tools. Here are the proper lengths:

Six 1 by 4s, 30"
Plywood ripped lengthwise at 32"
Four 1" dowels, 35⅛"
Two 1" dowels, 33 9/16"

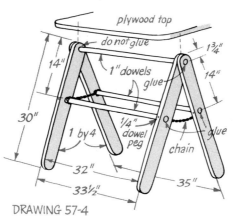

DRAWING 57-4

Set your compass at a 1¾" radius. Mark the half circles at the ends of all 1 by 4s and the quarter circles at the plywoods' four corners. Cut the rounded ends and corners.

Next, mark and drill the 1" holes according to drawing 57-4, centered and straight. Drill a test hole in a piece of scrap; make sure the dowels will push through it freely.

Assemble the sawhorses. If necessary, pound in the dowels, using a mallet or a hammer against a wooden block. Be sure the sawhorse legs are spaced correctly and the dowel ends go through the 1 by 4s. Then drill ¼" holes; glue and pound in ¼" dowel pegs to hold the 1" dowels in the legs (only into the outer 1 by 4s at the top dowel). Sand all surfaces until smooth.

Apply two coats of polyurethane and add the sash chains.

## Chimney flues & chopping block
*See facing page*

## Tile-top table
*See page 60*
*Design: Bill Provost*

## Oak nesting tables
*See page 61*
*Design: Sam Bateman*

# SMALL TABLE POTPOURRI

Small tables are invaluable. Without them, where would we put our coffee cups? Where would we place the sour cream dip for those celery sticks begging to be dunked? Where, every once in a while, would we park our feet?

Because they focus activity and attention, what better furnishing than a small table for displaying your individuality — for putting your creativity to work?

You can make a small table from practically anything that is flat, durable, and able to fit with your other furnishings. The three tables shown here to spark your imagination are only a sampling. You can see other small tables on pages 10, 15, 47, and 63. And most of the large table designs can be modified for smaller tables.

**Chimney flues** form the base for the chopping block table top. Buy flue tiles at a masonry supply; check home improvement stores for premade chopping blocks.

**The tile-top table** is quite long (about 5'). If you like the style but don't need a table this large, simply redesign it, modifying the size to fit the number and size of tiles you buy. You might also like to try some other modifications, such as making the legs from 4 by 4s, choosing other moldings, and fastening the parts together with dowels instead of bronze boat nails.

If you have a fairly complete shop or are involved in a woodworking class, you might like to try making the **oak nesting tables.** You'll find they challenge your skills and, when finished, will fit with practically any décor.

# Chimney flues & chopping block

*Simply buy the pieces and stack them together.*

(Photo on facing page)

**No tools required**

**Materials to buy:**
2 flue tiles, 8½" by 12"
1 hardwood chopping block, 2' by 4'
Clear polyurethane sealer

**HERE'S HOW:**
Just put the two flue tiles on end, spaced about 3' apart, and set the wooden chopping block across them.

If you wish, you can secure the block to the tiles by nailing a small wood scrap (about ¾" by 2" by 8") to the block's underside, just to the inside of each tile. But before you do, consider that most chopping blocks are good-looking on both sides: if the upper side ever gets marred or

stained, you can flip it over and use the underside.

You may decide not to use fasteners if you want to keep the table convertible. In fact, you may want to glue felt or fabric to the tiles' upper edges so they won't scratch the top's underside.

Finish the top by wiping on two coats of polyurethane sealer.

# Tile-top table

*Bold ceramic tiles offer a durable, handsome top.*

(Photo on page 58)

## Bare minimum tools:

Pencil
Measuring tape
Square
Compass
Four large C-clamps
Drill
Bit: 3/32"
Hammer
Coping saw
Sandpaper and finishing tools

## Helpful tools:

Saber saw
Miter box
Radial-arm saw
Power circular saw with plywood-
    cutting blade
Table saw

## Materials to buy:

2' by 8' piece of ¾" A-D plywood
2' by 8' piece of ½" ash veneer
17' of 2 by 2
8 ceramic tiles, 1' square
Mastic tile adhesive
Surface primer
Grout
18' decorative molding
Small box 6d common nails
Small box 2" boat nails
Small box 4d finishing nails
White glue
Wood filler
Stain
Clear polyurethane finish

## HERE'S HOW:

Begin by cutting out the 24" by 72" top base (D) from ¾" plywood (see drawing 60-4). Then cut out the ½" veneer pieces (A,B,C) according to the cutting diagram (drawing 60-2). Use drawing 60-3 to shape the (B) and (C) pieces.

Next, cut the 2 by 2s to the following lengths:

(E) Two 2 by 2s, 58"

(F) Two 2 by 2s, 14"
(G) Four 2 by 2s, 13"

Fasten the (E) and (F) pieces to the underside of the plywood base (D). Mark their placement according to drawing 60-1. Spread glue along

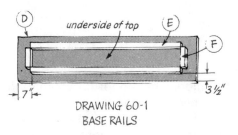

DRAWING 60-1
BASE RAILS

them, hold or clamp them in place, and secure by nailing with 6d nails from the plywood's face.

Next, position and secure the (B) and (C) panels to the legs (G). Do this one leg at a time, first gluing and clamping, then drilling pilot holes for the boat nails and hammering them in.

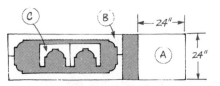

DRAWING 60-2 CUTTING DIAGRAM

When nailing, back the 2 by 2s with a brick or some other heavy object.

Next, set the plywood base (D) in position on the leg assembly, glue where the surfaces join, measure off and drill pilot holes, and pound in boat nails.

Sand the various wooden pieces (use only 400-grit paper on the veneers, removing very little wood).

Stain all wooden surfaces and let them dry. Fill gaps or mistakes with a wood filler that matches tne stain. Then apply the clear finish.

Next, glue and clamp down the center square of ½" veneer (A). Protect it from the clamps by laying a soft cloth across it and then laying a leftover scrap of ¾" plywood on top. Add short lengths of 2 by 4s to distribute the pressure evenly and apply the C-clamps, two on each side.

Now prime and spread mastic on the two ends of (D) where the tiles will go. Position the tiles and let the mastic dry. Then grout. Follow the manufacturer's directions for the tile.

Cut the decorative molding to encircle the table top's perimeter, mitering the corners. Check it for fit, stain it, and let it dry. Nail it on with 4d nails. Finish the table by applying the last coat of polyurethane to all wood parts.

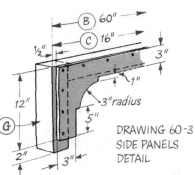

DRAWING 60-3
SIDE PANELS
DETAIL

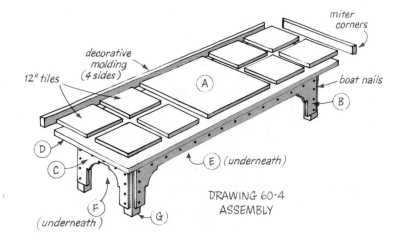

DRAWING 60-4
ASSEMBLY

# Oak nesting tables

*These stylish hardwood tables require woodworking skill and a few sophisticated tools.*

(Photo on page 58)

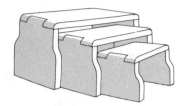

## Bare minimum tools:

Pencil
Measuring tape
Square
Coping saw
Handsaw or backsaw
Drill
Bit: ½″
Doweling jig
Hammer or mallet
Pipe or bar clamps
Half-round rasp and file
Sandpaper and finishing tools

## Helpful tools:

Band saw
Jointer
Radial-arm saw
Drill press
Router
Power sander

## Materials to buy:

11′ of 2″ by 9½″ hardwood
9′ of 2″ by 8″ hardwood
4′ of 2″ by 13″ hardwood
   (or 8′ of 2″ by 6½″)
3 hardwood dowels, ½″ by 3′
White glue
Wood filler
Clear polyurethane sealer
Wax

## HERE'S HOW:

Because hardwoods are seldom available in the broad widths necessary for these tables, you have to create the proper widths by gluing together two boards, edge-to-edge. (If you're lucky, you'll be able to find a 13-inch-wide board for the smallest table.)

To glue the boards together, follow the directions given on page 75 for gluing up table tops. Use drawing 61-1 for overall dimensions.

You'll need a jointer for planing the board edges perfectly flat. If you

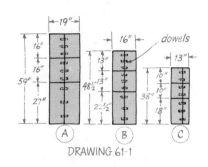

DRAWING 61-1

don't have one, look in the Yellow Pages for a cabinetmaker who does. While you're at it, choose a cabinetmaker who has a planer so you can return for the next step.

After gluing up the surfaces, take them to a planing mill or the cabinetmaker who has a planer. Have the slabs run through it, planing both sides to produce a finished thickness of 1¾″.

If you don't have the proper cutting tools, you can also have the cabinetmaker cut off the boards to the following lengths. (If you have the tools, do it yourself.)
1) Cut the 19-inch-wide slab to three lengths: two 16″ and one 27″.
2) Cut the 16-inch-wide slab to three lengths: two 13″ and one 22½″.
3) Cut the 13-inch-wide board to three lenghs: two 10″ and one 18″.

Next, mark the pieces for cutting the joints and curves as shown in drawings 61-2 and 61-3. Cut the tops to the proper widths. Also cut the side contours, using a coping saw or band saw.

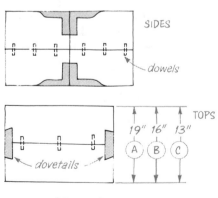

DRAWING 61-2
SIDE & TOP LAYOUTS

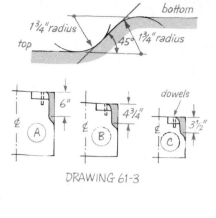

DRAWING 61-3

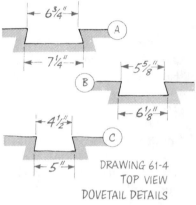

DRAWING 61-4
TOP VIEW
DOVETAIL DETAILS

Precisely mark the top dovetails as shown in the detail (drawing 61-4). Then cut them out — to the waste side of the line — using a backsaw or band saw.

Next, carefully file each joint to the exact dimension. Hold the top to the side pieces to mark for the side cuts; cut the sides the same way. Before gluing them, make sure the joints fit tightly and that the sides will be square with the tops.

Glue each joint, wiping off any excess. Clamp until dry. Then drill ½″ holes and insert dowels through

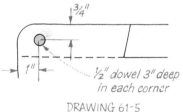

DRAWING 61-5
TOP VIEW OF CORNER

the board edges as shown in drawing 61-5. Pound in the dowels, cut them off flush, and sand the ends smooth.

Shape all corners and edges to a pleasing roundness, using a router or rasp and file. Fill any gaps or mistakes; sand each table until smooth. Apply the finish.

# SEE-THROUGH COFFEE TABLES

Even though a glass-topped coffee table offers plenty of surface, it doesn't visually crowd a room. Because it's transparent, the only mass you see is that of the table base.

Here are three good-looking bases you can try. The first two are quite easy to make; the third is a bit more challenging.

Though a base can be built for little money, glass adds considerably to the cost of a table. The thicker the glass, the more expensive; one square foot of ⅜" plate (float) glass costs about $8, ½" plate about $12, ¾" plate about $20. These prices include polished edges, but you'll have to pay more for any further work. Rounded corners or special shapes can raise the cost by $15 to $30.

These three tables have ½" glass tops — the minimum thickness you should use if edges or corners will be left exposed. If edges are enclosed and supported, ⅜" glass will do the job.

## Split chopping-block base

*Just cut the premade block in half and add dowels.*

(Photo on facing page)

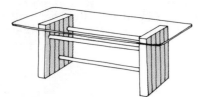

**Bare minimum tools:**

Pencil
Measuring tape
Square
Hammer
Drill
Bit: 1¼"
Sandpaper and finishing tools
Saw

**Helpful tools:**

Drill press
Radial-arm saw

**Materials to buy:**

30" by 15" by 2" chopping block
38" by 22" sheet of ½" plate glass*
3 hardwood dowels, 1¼" by 3'
Small rubber strips
White glue
Clear polyurethane sealer

*Specify polished edges.

**HERE'S HOW:**

If you don't own the proper cutting tools, have the lumberyard cut the dowels to length and the chopping block in half. The hardwood block isn't easy to cut by hand.

Next, drill the three holes in each block. If you don't have a drill press, visually align your drill with a square to keep it straight. Mark centers of holes where specified in drawing 64-1; then drill, using a 1¼" bit. When the bit's tip protrudes, flop the block and finish drilling from the other side.

Cut the dowels to 26" lengths and spread a little glue on the inner sides of the holes. Pound in the dowels until they poke through slightly;

(Continued on page 64)

## Split chopping-block base
*See facing page*
*Design: Bill Thompson*

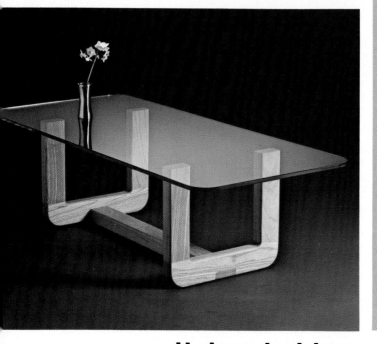

## Mahogany & tubing base
*See page 64*
*Design: Peter O. Whiteley*

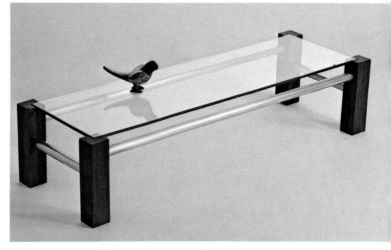

## U-shaped ash base
*See page 65*
*Design: Norman A. Plate*

. . . Continued from page 62

sand the ends flush with the block. Make sure the base sits level before the glue dries.

Finish the base with clear polyurethane sealer. Glue small rubber strips to the upper corners of each base and add the top.

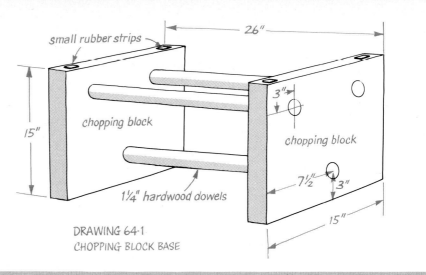

DRAWING 64-1
CHOPPING BLOCK BASE

# Mahogany & tubing base

## Making this base is as easy as cutting and drilling.

*(Photo on page 63)*

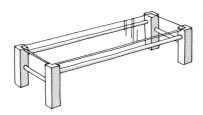

### Bare minimum tools:

Pencil
Measuring tape
Square
Handsaw
Hacksaw or tubing cutter
Drill
Bit: 1½"
C-clamps
Sandpaper and finishing tools

### Helpful tools:

Drill press
Radial-arm saw
Power sander

### Materials to buy:

20′ of 2 by 2 mahogany (1½" by 1½")
13′ of 1½" aluminum tubing
18" by 60" sheet of ½" plate glass*
White glue
Clear polyurethane finish

> *Specify polished edges. Take glass dimensions from base.

### HERE'S HOW:

Begin by cutting the pieces to size according to the following cutting schedule. You could have the wood cut at the lumberyard. If you do the cutting, use a square to mark and check the wood cuts. Cut the tubing with a hacksaw or a tubing cutter.

Twelve 2 by 2s, 14½"
Four 2 by 2s, 14"
Two 1½" aluminum tubes, 60"
Two 1½" aluminum tubes, 18"

Make each leg by gluing together four 2 by 2s (see drawing 64-2). Clamp them until dry. (Put scraps between clamps' jaws to keep them from denting the wood.)

When legs are dry, drill the 1½" holes in each where specified. Drill these holes 1½" deep.

Check the tubes for snug fit in the holes before gluing. If they are too tight to push all the way in, sand the holes slightly. Buff the tubes to a satin finish, using fine sandpaper. Spread glue on their ends, squirt a little glue in the holes, and then push the tubes into place.

Set the top on the base to be sure the table is square and the top will fit. Make any necessary adjustments; then let the glue dry.

Remove the top and sand the legs until smooth; add a clear finish. When the finish is dry, replace the top.

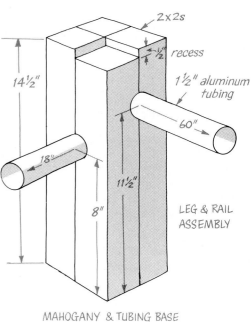

MAHOGANY & TUBING BASE
DRAWING 64-2

# U-shaped ash base

*For making this attention-getting base, you'll need sophisticated tools.*

(Photo on page 63)

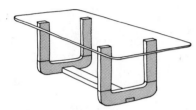

**Bare minimum tools:**

Pencil
Measuring tape
Square
Compass
Saber saw
Table saw
Drill
Bits: ⅝", #10 by 2" pilot
Bar or pipe clamps
Sandpaper and finishing tools

**Materials to buy:**

9' of 1¾" by 3½" ash
1 hardwood dowel, ⅝" by 36"
4 screws, 2" by #10
White glue
22" by 42" sheet of ½" plate glass*
Clear polyurethane finish

*Specify polished edges, 1½"
radiused corners.

**HERE'S HOW:**

Begin by cutting the ash to size, using a square to mark and check all cuts.

(A) Four pieces 10½" by 3" by 1¾"
(B) Two pieces 15¾" by 3½" by 1¾"
(C) One piece 29¾" by 3" by 1¾"
(D) Eight ⅝" dowels, 4" long

As shown in drawing 65-1, mark the radii for the bottom corners of the (B) pieces, using a compass set at 1½". Cut along the outside of the line with a saber saw or band saw.

Then set the table saw blade at a 1" height. Pass (B) pieces across the blade several times to cut 3-inch-wide notches at their centers. Reset the blade to a ¾" height and repeat the process to cut the rabbet in the ends of (C).

If you have a router or band saw, make a ½" cut in the top edge of both (B) pieces to form a shallow U shape.

Mark, drill, and dowel each leg (A) to the (B) pieces with two dowels (D) and glue at each joint. See more about doweling on page 74.

Round the edges of the various pieces. Use a router if you have one; otherwise, sand them until smooth.

Assemble (C) and (B) pieces. Drill pilot holes for 2" screws (two at each end) and screw the pieces together. Glue unless you want to be able to disassemble the table.

Sand the wooden surfaces and finish with clear polyurethane. Complete the table by setting the top in place.

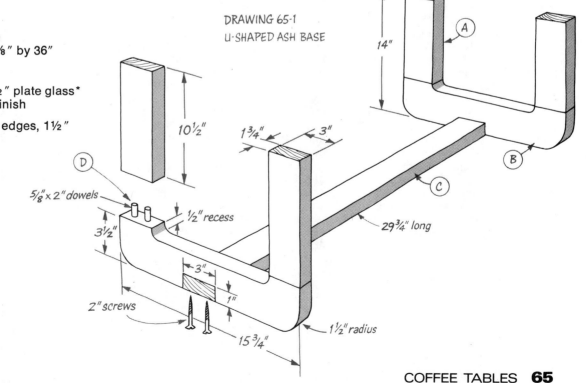

DRAWING 65-1
U-SHAPED ASH BASE

14"

10½"

1¾"  3"

29¾" long

⅝" x 2" dowels

½" recess

3½"

3"

1"

2" screws

15¾"

1½" radius

# TOOLS & TECHNIQUES

If how to dowel a joint or how to sew casings at the ends of a sling seems confusing, this section is for you. Here you'll find detailed information on the basic techniques needed for making many of this book's projects. Use this section as a reference — the wealth of tips gathered here can make woodworking an easier, more enjoyable experience.

First comes a section on how to size tables and chairs for maximum comfort and efficiency. Next, a primer on materials will simplify buying lumber. Then woodworking information begins: how to measure and mark, cut wood, drill, and assemble various parts. Here you will learn how to cut cleanly, drill straight, drive screws, make table tops, and much more. Following that is information on filling, sanding, and finishing wood. Ending the book is a section on making cushions and slings.

## Designing for comfort

Have you ever sat in a chair that looked inviting but, once you were seated, made you wish you were standing? Proof in point that a chair is more than something to look at. Because you sit on a chair, it must be comfortable or it loses its purpose. The same is true of a table — its height and size should make it comfortable to use.

Of course, chairs have varying purposes. We have lounges for snoozing, couches for group conversations, easy chairs for watching television, straight chairs for dining and working at tables, and many other seats that fall into less clearly defined categories. A chair's use should determine its proper angles and dimensions.

But comfort is relative to bodies. Though research has gathered measurements that are for "average" people, most of us aren't average in size or in any other way. We are male, female, tall, short, thin, fat, young, old, and with scores of other differences. Hardly average. And, though two people may be roughly the same height and weight, their proportions can differ. For example, the distance from their knees to their ankles may vary as much as 6".

Nevertheless, average dimensions give us something to work from. They are shown in drawings 66-1 and 67-1. But plan to measure the people who will actually be using the furniture and revise the dimensions accordingly.

In chair design, don't neglect support for the lower back (the lumbar region). Be sure to provide for firm support that will maintain

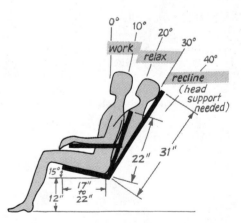

DRAWING 66-1

the natural S-curve of the spine. To feel the proper kind of support there, slip a rolled-up towel between your lower back and a chair — your back will welcome the relief of continual strain in that area.

Find more about comfort in the section on slings and cushions, beginning on page 77.

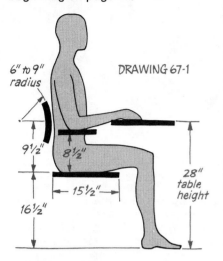

DRAWING 67-1

6" to 9" radius
9½"
8½"
28" table height
15½"
16½"

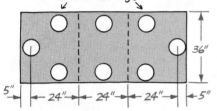

table settings

36"
5"
24"
24"
24"
5"

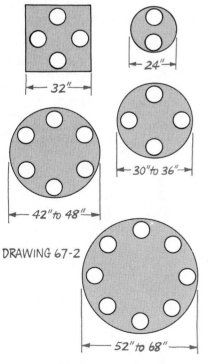

32"
24"
30" to 36"
42" to 48"
52" to 68"

DRAWING 67-2

TOP VIEW OF TABLES

# Lumber-buying basics

You're standing at the lumberyard's checkout counter. The cash register's numbers spin madly like cherries in a slot machine. You wait with bated breath. Then it happens— the total slams into view. You lose.

It's tough to win, but the surest bet for hedging your losses is to brief yourself before visiting the lumberyard. Know what to look for— lumber types, sizes, grades, and how they are sold. Carefully judge your requirements so you don't buy excessive amounts, wrong materials, or unnecessary quality. And most important, shop around. Make a list of your requirements and call several dealers for the best price.

To help you bridge the lumber-yard gap between your needs and what they cost, here is a basic lumber-buying primer.

### Hardwood or softwood?

Wood falls into two main categories: hardwoods and softwoods. Hardwoods come from deciduous trees, softwoods from conifers. Hardwoods are usually — but not always — harder than softwoods. One clear example is balsa. Though the softest of woods, it is classified a hardwood.

Standard lumber is softwood. What we call a "1 by 4" or "2 by 4" is usually pine or fir — two of the most commonly used softwoods. Both are good choices for making certain furniture pieces.

Fir is harder and stronger than pine but not nearly as strong as a hardwood like birch or oak. Because pine is probably the softest wood used in furniture making, it is also the easiest to work with for those who don't have many tools. It cuts easily and resists splintering.

Though most hardwoods are more expensive and harder to work than softwoods and though some must be specially ordered, they offer certain advantages. Most are very strong, have handsome grain and coloring, lend themselves to finely tooled joinery, and finish beautifully with more resistance to wear. Typically used hardwoods include oak, birch, ash, walnut, and teak. Of these, ash and birch are the least expensive, walnut and teak the most.

Hardwoods are the best choice where appearance is important, but because they're more expensive, don't use them where you don't need them.

### What quality?

Choose wood that is "kiln dried," straight, and flat. Stay away from wood that is bowed, twisted, or warped. And unless you want to choose knots and splits for effect, avoid them. By hand selecting your lumber, you can get better lumber for your money. Check out the lesser grades, working your way up until you find something suitable.

### What size?

Before you buy any softwood, know that *a 2 by 4 is not 2" by 4"*. Like all milled softwood lumber, it is given this size designation before it shrinks in drying and is planed to size. *A 2 by 4 is actually 1½" by 3½"*. The other nominal and actual sizes are shown in the chart below.

**STANDARD DIMENSIONS OF FINISHED LUMBER**

| SIZE TO ORDER | SURFACED (Actual Size) |
|---|---|
| 1 x 2 | ¾" x 1½" |
| 1 x 3 | ¾" x 2½" |
| 1 x 4 | ¾" x 3½" |
| 1 x 6 | ¾" x 5½" |
| 1 x 8 | ¾" x 7¼" |
| 1 x 10 | ¾" x 9¼" |
| 1 x 12 | ¾" x 11¼" |
| 2 x 3 | 1½" x 2½" |
| 2 x 4 | 1½" x 3½" |
| 2 x 6 | 1½" x 5½" |
| 2 x 8 | 1½" x 7¼" |
| 2 x 10 | 1½" x 9¼" |
| 2 x 12 | 1½" x 11¼" |

Thickness of 3" and 4" lumber is same as respective widths above.

*(Continued on page 68)*

Hardwood lumber is normally sold in odd lengths and sizes by the lineal foot, board foot, and sometimes by the pound. If you need hardwood for a particular project, specify the footage you need and ask the lumberman to sell you what he has in stock that will fill your requirements with the least waste. Again, if possible, hand pick your lumber.

In case you have to calculate board feet for ordering, here is the formula: thickness in inches times width in feet times length in feet equals the number of board feet. Use the nominal — not the actual — sizes. A 1 by 6 ten feet long would be computed $1'' \times 6/12' \times 10' = 5$ board feet. Another way to figure it is $1'' \times \frac{1}{2}' \times 10' = 5$ board feet.

## What about plywood?

Plywood, an excellent material, has several advantages over lumber: availability in large sheets, exceptional strength, high resistance to warp, and, in most cases, lower cost.

Though you'll have a hard time finding lumber over 12" wide, plywood comes in 4' by 8' sheets. These large sheets are excellent when you need large surfaces; for example, they eliminate the need for gluing together several boards to make a table top.

Plywood, like lumber, is divided into two categories: softwood and hardwood. In the case of plywood, the difference lies in the species of wood covering the outer faces of a panel.

Birch-veneered plywood is a good selection in the hardwood category. A handsome, light-toned wood, it is durable and one of the lowest-priced hardwood plywoods. Ash is another good low-cost choice. More expensive hardwood veneers include oak, walnut, and teak.

Plywood comes in a range of thicknesses: ⅛", 3/16", ¼", ⅜", ½", ⅝", ¾". The thicker it is, the more it costs, so save money by choosing the proper thickness.

In addition to wood-veneered panels, you can get softwood panels "resin-overlaid" or "density-overlaid." This means the plywood has a resin-impregnated paper permanently fused to its surfaces. Medium-density panels are excellent for painting; high-density panels are attractive even when left unfinished.

A word about plywood edges: when filled, sanded, and finished naturally, they can have a pleasing, "butcher block" laminated appearance. But if you'd rather not see the edges, mask them with veneer tape or moldings. Several alternatives are shown below. You can also paint plain edges.

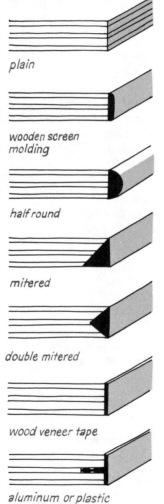

*plain*

*wooden screen molding*

*half round*

*mitered*

*double mitered*

*wood veneer tape*

*aluminum or plastic edging*

PLYWOOD EDGE TREATMENTS

# Measuring and marking

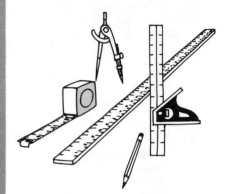

Most important in starting a project properly are careful measuring and marking. Because these are the first woodworking steps, they will set the stage for your finished project. By exact measuring and marking, you can avoid wasting time and materials and take the first step toward professional-looking results.

For most projects, you'll use a pencil, measuring tape, and combination square. For some projects, you'll also need a yardstick and a compass.

**Measuring.** Tight-fitting joinery requires measuring and cutting to within 1/32" or 1/64"; use a metal yardstick, tape measure, or square's blade. A tape measure's end hook should be loosely riveted so that it slides the distance of its own thickness, adjusting that thickness for precise "inside" and "outside" measurements.

Because measuring is easy and most materials are expensive, it pays to double check your measurements.

Whenever possible during construction, use one material to transfer measurements to another.

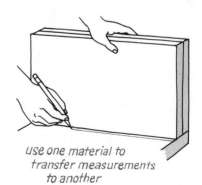

*use one material to transfer measurements to another*

**Marking lines.** A sharp pencil works well for drawing lines. Draw straight lines by guiding it along the edge of a square or straightedge. Draw curves or small circles using a compass.

For drawing large circles — like the top for a round table — tack one end of a yardstick to the material's center and, holding the pencil at the proper radius, revolve the yardstick like a large clock hand.

For marking straight across a board at 90° or at 45°, use a combination square.

**Checking for square.** Use a combination square for this purpose. Depending upon which side of the square's handle you use, you can check for true 90° or 45°.

Place the handle firmly along one of the board's side surfaces, sliding the blade into contact with the board end. If light shows between the blade and board, the end is not true. Check both directions. Plane or sand the dark ridges until the edge is square and no light shows through.

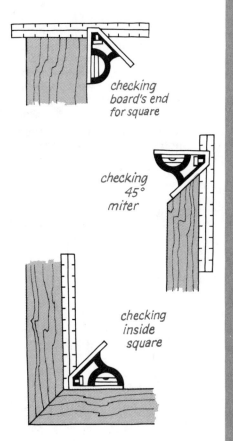

checking
board's end
for square

checking
45°
miter

checking
inside
square

# Cutting wood

In furniture making, cuts must be precise. They should be clean, square, and straight (unless they're supposed to be curved). When you join two pieces, no gaps should show between them.

For cutting properly, you need the right tools. What are the "right tools"? That depends totally upon the project.

Cutting tools vary from simple and inexpensive to sophisticated and costly. Generally speaking, hand tools are considerably less expensive than power tools. But some power tools — like saber saws and electric drills — come in inexpensive models that cost little more than their hand-powered counterparts.

Because a saber saw greatly simplifies both straight and curve cutting in materials up to about 1" thick, it is an excellent tool for making many of this book's projects.

Some projects require sophisticated tools, but there are ways of getting around buying them. Following are three alternatives.
• You can have cuts made at the lumberyard. Most lumberyards make straight cuts for a small fee. If you decide to do this, have them make the longest cuts. But before you do, find out how much it costs and whether or not they can cut precisely.
• Or you can join an adult education woodworking class. In many areas, high schools and colleges offer night classes on woodworking. These schools are usually equipped with excellent tools and very helpful instructors.
• One other alternative is to look up "Cabinet Makers" in the Yellow Pages and call two or three for cost estimates (you'll probably have to take your plans in for firm estimates).

**Miscellaneous cutting tools.** Though they don't fit the category of saws, such tools as chisels, planes, files, and the router are designed for cutting.

Chisels are used primarily for notching and cutting grooves (see "How to cut grooves"). They come in several sizes.

Planes slice off unwanted portions of wood, controlling a cut's width and depth. A block plane — the short one — cuts end grain well. A jack plane, about twice the length of a block plane, shears bumps and irregularities off a board's edges.

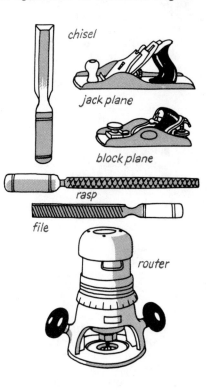

chisel

jack plane

block plane

rasp

file

router

Abrasive tools, such as files and rasps, remove small quantities of wood and make small areas smooth. They come in many shapes and sizes and with varying coarseness.

A router is versatile — it grooves, shaves, bevels, and rounds wood, depending upon the bit. This power tool cuts straight grooves, V-grooves, rounded grooves, and even exact dovetails. It can round or bevel the edge of a board in a single pass. Though rather expensive, routers can give projects a very finished look.

**How to make a clean cut.** The number of teeth per inch along a saw blade determines the kind of cut it makes. The more numerous the teeth, the smoother the cut. Choose blades that have 10 to 12 teeth per inch. For cutting smoothly with

*(Continued on page 70)*

. . . Continued from page 69

power saws, various kinds of plywood-cutting blades are made.

Where teeth exit, wood tends to splinter and break away. The kind of saw you use will determine the side of the wood that does this. Some saws have upward-cutting blades; others cut downward. If you're not sure, look to see the direction the teeth are pointed.

Cut good-side-up when using a handsaw, table saw, or radial-arm saw. If you use a portable circular saw or saber saw, cut the wood good-side-down. To minimize splintering, score along the cutting line's backside. Or try taping the line's backside with masking tape. Better yet, back the cut with a scrap pressed next to the piece you're cutting and cut both pieces together.

Don't forget to support both halves of the piece you're cutting. Otherwise, the saw will bind and, as you near the end of the cut, the unsupported piece will break away. If the saw binds anyway, stick a screwdriver in the end of the cut to spread it open.

**Sawing straight lines.** Several saws can cut straight lines: handsaw, saber saw, power circular saw, table saw, and radial-arm saw. The right methods for cutting straight depend upon the saw you use.

The key to cutting straight is using a guide. Of course, table saws and radial-arm saws have guides built in, but if you use a hand-held saw, you'll have to improvise one or use a small guide attachment.

Guide a handsaw against a board clamped along the cutting line. Start a cut by slowly drawing the saw *up* a few times to make a notch or "kerf." Then saw with short strokes at the blade's wide end, progressing to smooth, long, generous strokes, keeping your forearm in line with the blade. Saw lumber at a 45° angle; cut plywood and other sheet materials at 30°.

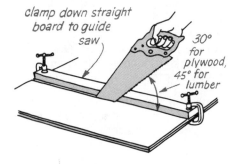

clamp down straight board to guide saw

30° for plywood, 45° for lumber

If you make a full kerf about ½" into the board's far edge, it will help guide the blade straight for the rest of the cut.

Saber saws usually come with a guide that is designed for making straight cuts a short distance from and parallel to a board's edge. When cutting across panels or wide surfaces, guide the saw's base plate against a straightedge clamped a measured distance from the cutting line. Keep the saw firmly against the guide, and continually check the blade to see that it doesn't bend away from the cut (it should stay vertically straight).

Wear eye protection when using a saber saw.

Power circular saws also come with guides for ripping narrow widths. But for cutting large panels, make a reusable guide from

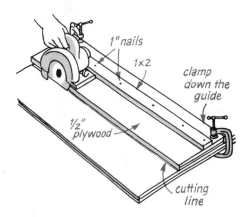

1" nails

1×2

clamp down the guide

½" plywood

cutting line

scrap plywood and molding as shown above. Work carefully and wear eye protection.

**Sawing curves and irregular lines.** Blades for sawing curves, zigzags, or irregular cuts must be thin, narrow in shape, and used in an almost straight up-and-down position. Saws suitable for this kind of cutting are the keyhole saw, coping saw, and saber saw.

The keyhole saw is the hand-powered version of the saber saw. It cuts curves and makes cutouts in the center of panels (but you have to start it from a drilled hole).

The coping saw, limited by its metal frame, cuts tightly curved lines. Its blades are removable. When cutting vertically in a vise,

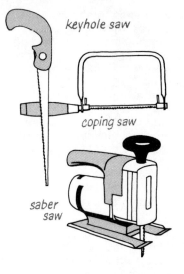

keyhole saw

coping saw

saber saw

point teeth toward the handle and cut on the pull stroke. If working on something supported horizontally, point the teeth away from the handle and cut on the push stroke.

The saber saw can do almost any kind of cutting. A great general purpose tool, it tracks curved lines easily. For greatest control, get a saber saw with a variable-speed trigger.

Using a saber saw, you can also dip into a panel's center to make a cutout by tilting the saber saw forward on its toe plate, starting the motor, and slowly lowering the tool. Do this with care. Wear eye protection when using power saws.

**How to cut a miter.** A miter is simply a through cut made at an angle — usually 45°. Mark the miter using a combination square; then cut it just as you would cut straight across the board, holding the saw at a slightly flatter angle. Use a fine-toothed saw and cut to the outside of the cutting line.

A great aid for cutting miters is a miter box. It supports small-dimensioned material securely and

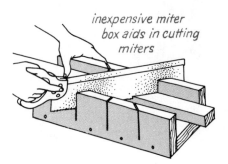

inexpensive miter box aids in cutting miters

guides the saw for precise cuts.

Radial-arm saws and table saws are excellent for cutting exact miters.

**How to cut grooves.** Grooves are probably the most difficult kind of cuts to make, especially when you're using hand tools. The trick is to cut a wide groove with a flat base.

Power tools cut grooves easily. The best tools are routers and power saws equipped with dado blades. You just guide them across the surface — the bits or blades do all the work. Or, using a power saw with a regular blade, you can make a series of joined cuts within the area to be removed. You can also get an inexpensive attachment for a power drill that cuts grooves to about 1″ deep (check your hardware store).

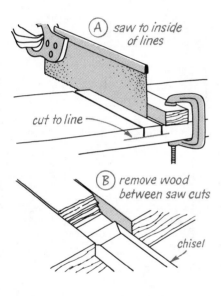

Ⓐ saw to inside of lines

cut to line

Ⓑ remove wood between saw cuts

chisel

To cut a groove using hand tools, first mark the groove; then saw to the inside of the lines as deep as you want the groove. If it's a very wide cut, saw a couple extra cuts across the waste wood in the middle. Then, using a chisel, remove the waste wood.

If the groove doesn't extend to the board's edges, cut it using a chisel. Lightly rap the chisel on each across-grain mark (bevel facing waste wood) to keep the wood from splitting beyond those marks. Then make a series of parallel cuts to the desired depth, moving with the blade's bevel forward. Keep the chisel almost vertical to the surface.

Hand holding the chisel and decreasing its angle considerably, chip out all the waste wood. Make

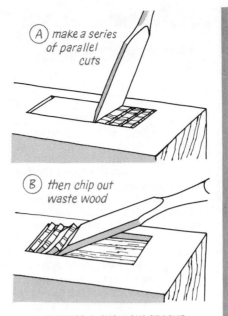

Ⓐ make a series of parallel cuts

Ⓑ then chip out waste wood

CUTTING A SHALLOW GROOVE USING A CHISEL

final smoothing cuts with the chisel's bevel almost flat against the wood.

For a deep groove, first remove excess wood by drilling a series of holes. Then join the holes and square up the resulting mortise using a chisel.

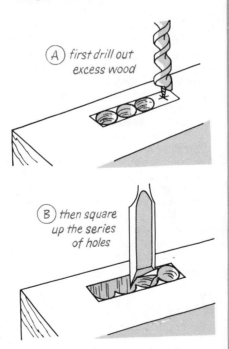

Ⓐ first drill out excess wood

Ⓑ then square up the series of holes

MAKING A DEEP MORTISE

# Drilling properly

For many of this book's projects, you'll need a drill. Though hand drills can do most of the work, a ¼″ or ⅜″ power drill is highly recommended. It makes the job of drilling much faster and easier and, with an abundance of available attachments, can become one of the most used tools in your tool box.

Four drilling problems crop up often: 1) Centering the moving drill bit on its mark, 2) Drilling a hole straight, 3) Keeping the wood's backside from breaking away as the drill bit pierces, and 4) When drilling to a measured depth, knowing when to stop. Following are some techniques that will help rid your work of these problems.

For information on drilling pilot holes and countersinking, see "How to drive screws," page 73.

**How to center the bit.** Keep a pointed tool handy for center punching. A couple of taps with a hammer on a large nail, nailset, or punch will leave a hole that will prevent the bit from wandering.

**How to drill straight.** A drill press or press accessory for your hand drill offers the best means for drilling holes straight. But if you don't have one of these, you'll have to try something else. Three methods are shown below. You can use a commercially available drill guide for twist bits, make a guide by predrilling a scrap block of wood, or use a square to visually align the drill.

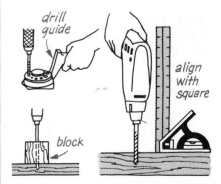

drill guide

block

align with square

(Continued on page 72)

... Continued from page 71

**How to drill cleanly.** To keep a drill bit from breaking out the wood's backside, do one of two things: 1) Lay or clamp a wood scrap firmly against your workpiece's backside

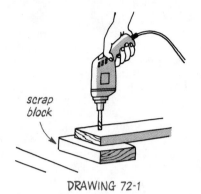

DRAWING 72-1

and drill through the workpiece into the scrap as shown in drawing 72-1, or 2) Just after the drill's point pierces, flop over the workpiece and finish drilling from the other side.

**How to gauge depth.** To stop a drill bit at the right depth, put a piece of

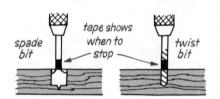

DRAWING 72-2

tape around the shank as shown in drawing 72-2.

**General drilling tips.** Clamp materials down, particularly when using a power drill — the torque, when combined with a large bit, can easily wrench the wood from your grasp. Hold the drill firmly, leaving the motor on until the bit is withdrawn from the wood. To avoid breaking small bits, don't tilt the drill once the bit has entered the wood. Wear plastic safety goggles, especially when drilling brittle surfaces.

# Joinery and fastening techniques

After marking, cutting, and drilling pieces, the next logical step is joinery — fastening the pieces together to form a finished project. Though wood can be cut to form dozens of kinds of joints, the methods of fastening those joints are few: gluing, clamping, nailing, screwing, or bolting. This section tells how to use fasteners and how to make basic joints.

Basic fastening tools are shown in drawing 72-3. They are all relatively inexpensive hand tools. Of course, a saw is needed for cutting most types of joints; saws are discussed on page 69 under "Cutting wood."

**Gluing and clamping.** One of the best fasteners for permanent joints is glue. Glue strengthens almost all joints. Unless you use contact cement or epoxy (depending upon what you are gluing), clamp the joint after applying glue. C-clamps, bar clamps, or pipe clamps will handle most standard clamping jobs.

Most of this book's projects specify white glue. It has moderate moisture resistance and strength; it works well on wood and is easy to use. Spread it on the adjoining surfaces, clamp them tightly together, wipe off the excess, and let dry according to label recommendations. Be sure to wipe off the excess — most stains and transparent finishes will not take to glue-coated areas.

Choose and use other kinds of glue according to their labels.

C-clamps work well for miscellaneous clamping jobs. They come in sizes with openings from 3″ to 16″. Protect wooden surfaces from being damaged by a metal clamp's jaws by slipping a scrap block between the jaws and the wood before tightening the clamp.

Bar clamps and pipe clamps work well for clamping across broad surfaces. Bar clamps open as far as the bar part of the clamp allows. Pipe clamps depend for their maximum spread upon the length of pipe you attach them to.

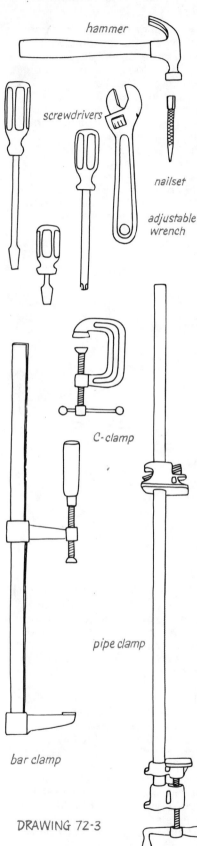

DRAWING 72-3

**How to nail.** Nailing is easy, inexpensive, and fast. It works fine where only medium strength is needed — but use glue, too. Never expect nails to hold a chair's primary joints or other joints where nails might work loose.

Though nails with sharp points hold better than blunt ones, they tend to split wood. Blunt the point with a tap of the hammer before driving a nail into wood that splits easily. And don't line up two nails

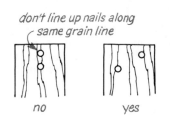

*don't line up nails along same grain line*

no          yes

along the same grain lines in the board — the wood will probably split. Instead, stagger nails slightly.

When starting a nail, hold it near its head. That way, if you miss, you'll only knock your fingers away. Once the nail is started, let go of the nail and swing the hammer with fuller strokes, squarely hitting the nail's head. Visualize a pivot point at the handle's end and keep that point level with the nail head.

Where you are concerned about the wood's appearance, don't crush the surface with the last few hammer blows. Instead, use a nailset to set the nail heads below the surface about 1/16″. Then fill the holes.

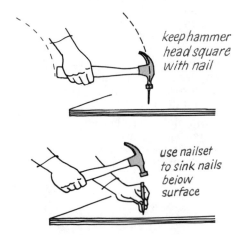

*keep hammer head square with nail*

*use nailset to sink nails below surface*

When pulling a nail, put a scrap block under the hammer's head so you won't damage the surface.

**How to drive screws.** Though screws are slightly more difficult and time-consuming to drive than nails, they are considerably stronger — especially when supplemented with glue. When used without glue, screws can be removed, creating a demountable joint.

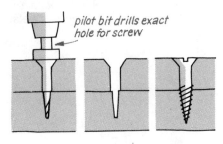

*pilot bit drills exact hole for screw*

Drill pilot holes for screws. Either select a drill bit that's slightly smaller than the screw's shank or use a "pilot bit." As shown in the drawing above, this bit drills a hole that's just the right shape for a particular screw. Some bits are adjustable; others match one screw size. The latter type is the most reliable.

When screwing into the end grain of wood, it's a good idea to first drill

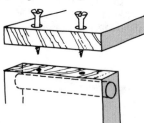

*insert a dowel when screwing into end grain*

a hole and insert a hardwood dowel. This gives the screws something strong to grip.

Choose a screwdriver that fits the screw's slot, not one that's too small or too large. And don't work with a burred or bent screwdriver.

Where you don't want screw heads to show, countersink them below the wood's surface; then fill the hole above the head with putty or a wooden plug. For a wooden plug, drill the countersinking hole from ⅛″ to ⅜″ deep and, instead of doweling, use a "plug-cutter" bit to cut the plug from a scrap of the same wood. This way, the plug's grain and color will match that of the wood you're plugging.

**How to use bolts.** Unlike a screw, which digs into wood, a bolt has a threaded shaft that grips a nut. Because it grips the nut — not the wood — a bolt is very strong and doesn't chew up the wood when removed.

Several types — with varying kinds of heads—are available. Some you tighten with a screwdriver, others with a wrench. You drive a hanger bolt by running a couple of nuts on the shaft, tightening them together, and then driving the top nut with a wrench.

You can countersink bolt heads the same way you'd countersink a screw (see "How to drive screws," at left), but do not countersink carriage bolts if you want the bolts removable (otherwise you can't get a tool under the bolt's head).

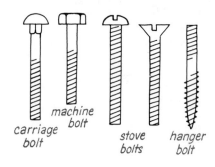

*carriage bolt*   *machine bolt*   *stove bolts*   *hanger bolt*

*hex nut*          *square nut*

*wing nut*         *T-nut*

*cap ("acorn") nut*

Several kinds of nuts are available. The kinds most used for this book's projects are hex nuts, cap nuts, wing nuts, and T-nuts. Fitting flush on a surface, T-nuts provide metal threads in a hole. A T-nut is strong only when pulled from the side of the hole opposite its body — it can't withstand a pull from the same side.

*(Continued on page 74)*

*. . . Continued from page 73*

**How to make a butt joint.** Measure the pieces and mark them with a 90° square. Cut them carefully so they

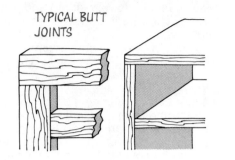

TYPICAL BUTT JOINTS

won't show gaps. Add glue and clamps and/or fasteners like screws, nails, or dowels.

**How to make a miter joint.** Measure the pieces, remembering that they both must go the full distance to the corner. Mark them, using a 45°

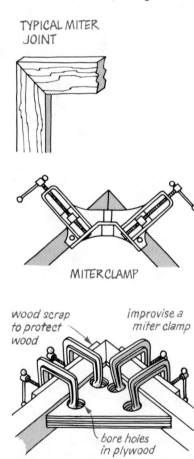

TYPICAL MITER JOINT

MITER CLAMP

wood scrap to protect wood

improvise a miter clamp

bore holes in plywood

angle, and cut carefully. Apply glue to the two joining surfaces and clamp, using a special clamp made for this purpose or improvising one as shown above. For strength, add fasteners.

**How to make a dowel joint.** You'll encounter two different kinds of dowel joints: one is quite easy to make; the other is more difficult, requiring special tools and careful drilling.

The first one involves cutting a basic butt joint, joining the two pieces by holding or clamping them together, drilling holes *through* one and into the other, scoring dowels,

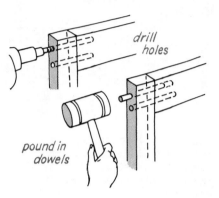

drill holes

pound in dowels

coating them with glue, coating the two meeting surfaces with glue, and pounding the dowels in from the outside.

The other method—perhaps more common — is blind doweling. With this method, the dowels don't show. Instead, you mark and drill separate matching holes in the two meeting halves, push dowels into one of the halves, add glue, and then fit together the two halves.

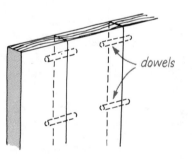

dowels

The tough part is getting the holes to match exactly and drilling them straight (see page 71). A tool — called a "doweling jig" — is made especially for this purpose. Clamp this tool onto one of the surfaces and drill through the guide holes. Then clamp the adjoining surface in place, unclamp the first piece, and

*doweling jig aids in drilling dowel holes*

drill the matching holes in the second surface.

Or you can mark the two pieces as shown below. Do your best to drill the holes straight (see page 71).

You can also use "dowel centers." To do this, drill the holes in one of the surfaces, put the centers in the

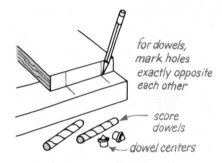

for dowels, mark holes exactly opposite each other

score dowels

dowel centers

holes, and push the other piece in place against the first one. The dowel centers mark the exact place to drill.

Before pounding in dowels, cut them slightly shorter than the combined depth of the matching holes. Then, after scoring small grooves along the dowels so glue can escape the holes, spread glue along them. Insert them, put together the two halves, and clamp the joint tight.

**How to make a spline joint.** A wooden spline, inserted in a saw kerf, is a strong and simple way to strengthen miter and butt joints.

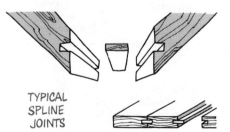

TYPICAL SPLINE JOINTS

To be sure the grooves match, use the same table saw or router setting to cut them. A spline's width should be slightly less than the combined depth of kerfs. For most work, a good spline size is ¼" thick by 1¼" wide. For this, you'd cut a groove ¼" wide and about 11/16" deep in each meeting piece.

Cut the spline, spread glue along it, and put it in place in one of the grooves. Push the other half in place and clamp.

**How to make an interlocking joint.** The simple slide-together joints shown in drawing 75-1 are used for several of this book's projects. Flat interlocking joints between boards may require fasteners, but long-slot interlocking joints for plywood panels — like those used in the plywood chair on page 22 — work well without fasteners. And you can disassemble them by simply sliding them apart.

To make them, cut matching grooves in the two pieces. A groove's width should be exactly the same as the connecting piece's width. Normally, the grooves' depths are figured to intersect midway

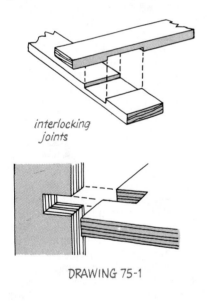

*interlocking joints*

DRAWING 75-1

between the two pieces.

Mark for the grooves, using the joining piece as a guide. Then cut the grooves as explained under "How to cut grooves" on page 71.

# How to glue-up a table top

You can make a table top from plywood or some other material that comes in broad panels. But because lumber comes only in sizes up to about 12" wide, to make a solid-wood table top you'll need to join together several boards edge to edge.

One alternative to making a table top is to buy a premade butcher block top, sold at building supply stores and by some furniture stores.

Following are ways to glue-up your own butcher block style table tops.

**Preparation.** Cut the boards to ½" or 1" longer than the table top's finished length to allow for final squaring and trimming. The board edges should be perfectly flat, square, and sharp cornered. This means that, prior to buying the lumber, you should have had it run through a jointer. Otherwise, you'll have to run the boards through a jointer or table saw to square up the edges.

If you don't have the proper tools for this, call a few cabinetmakers or a local planing mill to get cost estimates.

After cutting, lay the planks side by side with the grain of all planks running in the same direction. Also check the end grain of each plank— the direction of annual rings should alternate (see drawing 75-2) to minimize warping. Once you've arranged the planks, number them and mark "face" on the upper surface of each.

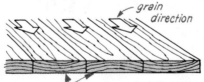

*grain direction*

*alternate ring directions*

DRAWING 75-2

If you plan to dowel or spline the top together—the most professional method — you'll need to have a few bar or pipe clamps on hand. These must be long enough to span all the widths of lumber you use.

**Joining boards with splines.** If you have a table saw or router, it's easier to use splines to join the planks than it is to use dowels. For splines, one long groove along the edge of a

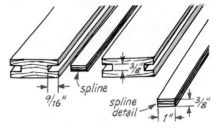

*spline*

*spline detail*

DRAWING 75-3

board has to match another board's long groove. But when you use dowels instead, several dowels must line up exactly—a more challenging and time-consuming job.

For splines, use 1" strips of ⅜" plywood. Cut grooves in the joining halves 9/16" deep and ⅜" wide, down the middle of the board edges.

To keep the splines from showing at the table's ends, stop the grooves about 2" short of the board ends.

Set the saw or router guide and cut all boards before adjusting the guide for second cuts. Using a table saw, either saw with a dado blade that makes a ⅜" cut or make three or four parallel passes using a regular blade. If you saw using a regular blade, make one pass along all boards, change the saw setting, make the second pass along all boards, and so forth. This way, all grooves will match.

Cut the splines the same length as the grooves. Spread glue along the splines and the groove's inner sides.

Insert the splines in the grooves, push all the planks together, and position the clamps, placing one about every 18". Slip a scrap of wood under the clamp's jaws to guard against marring the wood. Before applying maximum pressure, sandwich the top with 2 by 4s and C-clamps as shown in drawing 75-4. This will keep the boards from buckling. Wipe away excess glue and let dry completely before removing clamps.

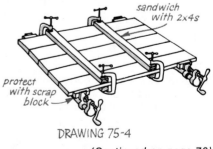

*sandwich with 2x4s*

*protect with scrap block*

DRAWING 75-4

(Continued on page 76)

... Continued from page 75

**Joining boards with dowels.** Begin by clamping together two adjoining boards as shown in drawing 76-1. Using a square, mark dowel holes, allowing 6 inches between them except at the ends, where dowels should set about 3 inches from the trim lines. For 1½" thick material, use ⅜" dowels.

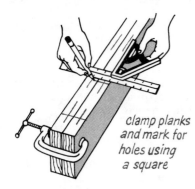

clamp planks and mark for holes using a square

DRAWING 76-1

Drill the holes straight as described under "How to drill straight" on page 71.

Cut the dowels a fraction shorter than the combined depth of the two matching holes; then score them so glue can escape. Brush edges of the planks with glue, allowing some to run into holes, and coat the dowels. Pound them into the holes in one side of all the planks (drawing 76-2); then drive the opposing planks onto the doweled planks with light mallet or hammer blows, protecting the planks by hitting a

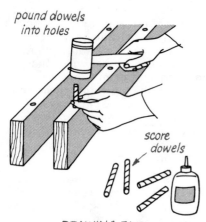

pound dowels into holes

score dowels

DRAWING 76-2

wooden block held against their edges. Don't knock in just one place — work all the way across.

Clamp the boards, using the same methods described on page 75 under "Joining boards with splines."

**Joining planks with threaded rods.** For this method you don't need clamps, but you do need a drill bit long enough to drill edgewise through the boards. Too, a doweling jig, for drilling straight, is almost a necessity. Threaded rods, running through holes drilled in the board edges, cinch them together. (See drawing 76-3.)

Buy ½" diameter threaded rods that are as long as the combined width of all planks. Two threaded rods will pull together tables under 5 feet long; you'll need three rods for tables up to 8 feet long. Mark the planks for drilling, using the same methods shown for marking dowel holes (drawing 76-1).

Drill 9/16" or ⅝" holes. And where each hole shows at the table top's outer edges, drill a 1" hole for countersinking a washer, nut, and wooden plug.

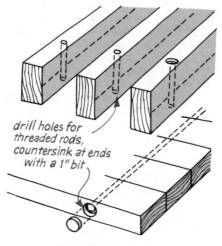

drill holes for threaded rods, countersink at ends with a 1" bit

DRAWING 76-3

After drilling all holes, slide the rods through to check for fit. Also check rod lengths — if they're too long, use a hacksaw to cut them (don't forget to allow for the wooden plugs). Pull out the rods. Put a washer and nut on one end of each rod; then slide the rods through the first end plank.

Brush glue generously on the inner edge of the plank and slide the second plank onto the rods and against the first plank. Continue until all planks are in place. Add washers and tighten on nuts, using a socket wrench. Wipe off excess glue. Cut wooden plugs and glue them in the holes.

When the glue is dry, trim the table ends to exact size. Sand the surface flat (see the following discussion of "Sanding the top").

**Making a nail-together top.** No clamps are needed for making this kind of laminated top — it's glued together in a very simple way. But you can't use broad planks; you have to make the table from 1 by 2s or 2 by 2s.

If you use softwood, have the rounded edges planed square (or rip 2 by 4s in half). Either way, point

glue and nail together 1 by 2s or 2 by 2s

DRAWING 76-4

the squared edges upward. Working on a flat surface, start at the middle and edge-glue one board to another, nailing it every 8" using 8d finishing nails as shown in drawing 76-4.

Work progressively outward from this middle pair, gluing and nailing through the edges that will be hidden. Be sure to keep all pieces flat and wipe away excess glue. When you get to the last two outside boards, set the nailheads below the surface and fill the holes.

**Sanding the top.** A laminated top needs a lot of sanding before it can be smooth and flat. For those put together without metal fasteners, you might try the following alternative to excessive hand or belt sanding. Locate a planing mill, millwork shop, or large lumberyard that has a drum sander large enough to receive your table top. Get prices for the job of sanding your top. Chances are good that sanding it perfectly smooth by sending it through the drum sander two or three times will cost less than $10. But don't have them sand a top that has metal fasteners — these could tear or damage the belts, costing you a lot more. If this easy alternative doesn't work out for you, sand the top until flat and smooth, using the methods that follow.

# Finishing wood

Wood should be given a finish to protect it from being soiled, stained, or dented. In addition, a finish can enhance the appearance of most woods. But before applying a finish, prepare the wood by filling holes and imperfections and sanding it smooth.

**Filling holes.** Before filling wood, consider the finish you plan to apply. Don't use a filler that's going to stick out like a sore thumb. Of course, if you plan to paint the project, practically any filler will work — the paint should cover all.

For natural finishes, fill blemishes, using wood dough or stick shellac (a specialty product for furniture makers). Both products come in colors that match most woods.

Spread wood dough with a putty knife; melt stick shellac into the hole or crack. Always build up the patch slightly above the surface and then sand off the excess. When patching large holes, fill the hole, let the compound dry, sand the surface on and around the patch, and repeat the process.

Whether you're applying a natural finish, staining, or painting, seal knots with shellac before finishing— this will prevent sap from seeping through.

When staining you should use a slightly different treatment. Because fillers don't dry at the same porosity as woods, they often show up under stains — the stain gets absorbed unevenly. So choose a wood dough that is close to the wood's finished color and apply it *after* the stain.

You can touch up with stain if necessary, and apply a finish coat of clear polyurethane. First test the color match on a piece of extra wood. You'll find that dark stains and opaque stains usually camouflage fillers best.

**Sanding wood.** Though sanding is sometimes a tedious job, it can give your project that professional touch. So don't neglect it — after working hard at making a project, it doesn't pay to scrimp with the part that shows the most.

A power sander makes sanding easy, but unless you have an enormous amount of sanding to do, you won't need one. Though hand sanding takes elbow grease, it produces a fine finish.

If you have one, a belt sander can

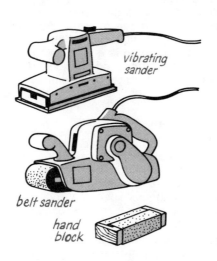

*vibrating sander*

*belt sander*

*hand block*

remove a lot of wood fast. Use it only *in line* with the wood's grain. Graduate from coarse to fine sanding belts, but be careful — a coarse belt on a belt sander can devour your project.

Vibrating sanders work more like hand sanding. Some move the sandpaper in an "orbiting" motion; others back and forth. For final sanding use only the kind that works back and forth.

Whether you sand by hand or power, divide the process into three steps: rough, preparatory (after you've filled defects), and finish. Rough-sand with 80-grit sandpaper; preparatory-sand with 120-grit; and finish-sand with 180-grit (or finer). A final hand sanding usually improves a finish's appearance. Prior to finishing, remove dust, using a rag moistened with mineral spirits.

**Applying the finish.** Most projects in this book recommend polyurethane as a finish. Available in both pigmented and clear, it is durable and easy to apply with a rag.

Three kinds are available: gloss, satin, and penetrating sealer. Gloss and satin lie on the surface, giving it a plastic-coated appearance. Gloss, of course, is shinier than satin. Penetrating sealer soaks into the wood, protecting it from within. Choose this kind for maximum highlighting of wood texture.

Hundreds of varnishes, lacquers, oils, stains, enamels, and other finishes are available. Find out more about these from your dealer.

# How to make cushions and slings

After you've sat in a hard, flat seat for an hour, it gets uncomfortable. Why? Because it restricts blood flow to your tissues. A fabric sling or a cushion, on the other hand, will "give" slightly to fit your contours, offering considerably more comfort. The following pages tell you how to make comfortable cushions and slings.

Slings are discussed first. Because they are lightweight, inexpensive, and easy to make, they appear in most of this book's seating projects — both as the seat alone and as a support for cushions.

Then cushions are discussed. In this section you'll find information on choosing and working with foam and other stuffings, choosing upholstery fabrics, and cushion shapes and how to make them.

## SLINGS

A sling is simply a piece of strong fabric—usually canvas or leather—stretched across a seat frame. Because the fabric stretches around your contours, it offers comfort — though not quite as much as a cushion. Slings in this book's projects are fastened to the frames by several methods.

You can attach a sling permanently to a frame by fastening it at each end with upholstery tacks, as was done with the chairs on page 23. Although this is the easiest method, cleaning permanently attached slings once they're dirty is a near impossibility.

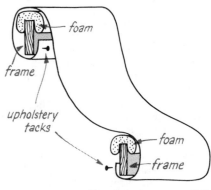

*foam*

*frame*

*upholstery tacks*

*foam*

*frame*

*(Continued on page 78)*

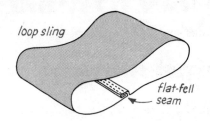

loop sling

flat-fell
seam

Or you can make one huge loop, such as the one on the hanging tube chair on page 26. The two fabric ends were joined with a flat-fell seam. To do this, seam the two pieces together about ⅝″ from their ends. Press the joined ends down to one side; then trim the lower seam allowance to ¼″. Curl the top seam allowance under it about ⅛″ and pin. Topstitch it close to the fold; then turn it right side up and topstitch close to the seam for added strength.

The most commonly used method to attach a sling is to sew a casing (loop) along each end of the sling. You push the casing through a slot in the wooden frame and run a dowel or rod through the casing so it can't be pulled back through the slot (see the two chairs on page 34).

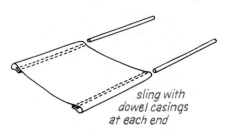

sling with
dowel casings
at each end

Because you usually finish fabric edges before making a casing, edge-finishing information appears below, followed by the techniques for making casings. When figuring fabric requirements, allow for seam allowances and casings where required. Choose heavy-duty thread and double stitch for strength.

When the sling will be seen from both sides, finish the edges so fraying won't show. Do this by first folding under ¼″, then folding under another ¼″, then pinning. Stitch along the resulting triple thickness.

Make a casing by figuring the necessary loop size, folding over the end to create that size loop, tucking the unfinished fabric edge under the fold about ¼″, and stitching along it.

## CUSHIONS

A cushion is generally a fabric bag filled with something soft — usually polyurethane foam or more expensive foam rubber. Some cushions have foam cores that are wrapped with one or more layers of polyester batting, a thick, fluffy fabric. Following is a discussion of stuffings, fabrics, and methods of combining them to form comfy cushions.

### Cushion stuffings

The cushions described in this book's projects recommend particular stuffings. The various stuffings are discussed here; you can vary them, depending upon the appearance you want the cushions to have.

**Foam blocks.** Most firm, flat, squared-off cushions have one-piece or layered foam-block fillings. Foam blocks come in thicknesses of 1″ increments. They are sold by the square foot. Price depends upon size, density, amount of necessary cutting, and, most of all, the type of foam. There are two kinds: polyurethane foam ("polyfoam") and foam rubber.

Polyfoam is much cheaper than foam rubber but lacks durability, breaking down in sunlight and with usage. Foam rubber weighs more. Both come in four densities: super-soft, soft, medium, and dense. Foam rubber tends to be firmer in like classifications: a "soft" foam rubber is usually about the same density as a "medium" polyfoam.

Most cushions are made up from two or more densities. Commonly, a seat cushion has a medium or dense foam core sandwiched by two outer layers (about 1″ thick) of soft foam. A typical back cushion is made the same way but has outer layers of super-soft foam. Additionally, cushions with a soft, rounded look usually are wrapped with at least one layer of batting.

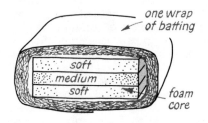

one wrap
of batting

soft
medium
soft

foam
core

TYPICAL SEAT CUSHION

Buy precut blocks at large yardage stores or upholstery supply shops. For custom sizes or styles, visit an upholstery shop or foam dealer. To find foam dealers, look in the Yellow Pages under "Rubber — Foam & Sponge."

Working with foam is easy. Use a serrated bread knife or — even better — an electric carving knife to cut it. For maximum cutting ease, spray the knife's blade with a silicone or nonstick vegetable coating. For gluing together various foam pieces, buy from a foam dealer easy-to-use foam adhesive made for the purpose.

**Foam bolsters and pillows.** Polyfoam and foam rubber also come in precut pillow forms and in cylindrical bolsters. Bolsters, specified for several of this book's projects, are sold by foam density and by bolster diameter and length.

**Shredded foam.** The most obtainable form of cushion stuffing — shredded foam — is sold in yardage, notion, and variety stores. Basically, it is the same as the foam discussed above under "Foam blocks," but it has been chopped into small chunks by a shredder. Shredded foam is cheap and easy to stuff into a fabric form; those are practically its only attributes. It looks and feels lumpy, doesn't hold a particular shape, and is messy. If you plan to stuff a cushion with shredded foam, consider making an inner bag of muslin so you can easily remove the cover for cleaning.

**Polyester batting.** This is a synthetic with the feel of fluffy cotton. In cushion making, it's most commonly wrapped around foam blocks to soften and round them. For this, it's sold by the yard and has a muslin backing. It is also sold in loose bulk form for completely stuffing cushions and in bed-size sheets for padding quilts.

Super-soft foam does the main softening of a cushion best. Use the batting — at most two or three wraps — to round edges and give a cushion loft. Batting settles with use. If you overwrap cushions, they may "deflate" in time.

To give cushion edges and corners a very round effect, first trim the foam at an angle along the edges and then wrap. To soften all edges, wrap from front to back and from side to side.

Secure wrapped batting to the foam by handstitching the loose end to the batting layer beneath it.

## Choosing a fabric

When selecting an upholstery fabric, you'll perhaps consider its appearance first of all. But this is not the only factor to think about. Here are a few other considerations:

**Texture.** Coarse fabrics snag clothing and are uncomfortable to sit on if you're wearing thin clothing. Slippery fabric slides you away from back support. Choose fabrics that can breathe; if they can't, you'll perspire.

Textured fabrics with a nap — such as velvet, fake fur, and some types of suede cloth — have to be sewn with all the nap going in one direction. Sometimes this means buying extra fabric.

**Washability.** Washable fabrics are generally more desirable than those that need to be dry cleaned. Even better for maintenance are fabrics with spot-resistant finishes, soil-release finishes, and permanent-press finishes.

You should preshrink washable fabrics. Do this the same way you'll wash and dry the finished cover.

**Patterned fabrics.** Before buying a print or striped fabric, visualize it on the completed project. If you choose a striped fabric, decide the stripes' direction and determine whether you'll need extra fabric for matching the stripes. For patterned fabrics, plan to direct the pattern one way and decide whether or not to match it. Compensate for this when figuring yardage.

## Cushion shapes

A cushion isn't hard to define — it's just stuffing held by a fabric bag. The way you sew together the bag will make a difference in the cushion's shape. A discussion of the main types and how to make them follows.

A word about preparation: decide your method before buying the fabric — it can make a difference in the necessary amount.

Preshrink the fabric (if washable) and cut it out according to the pattern given in the project how-to.

In the construction, don't forget to allow for an opening that's large enough to push the stuffing through. And decide how you'll close that opening. If you use a zipper, hook-and-pile tape, or upholstery tape with snaps, install the device according to manufacturer's directions while the cover is inside out.

KNIFE-EDGE CUSHION

**Knife-edge cushions.** Drawing above shows an example of a knife-edge cushion. This style cushion is used for the couch on page 15, the tubing chair on page 31, and the backbone beanbag on page 7. Knife-edge cushions are quite easy to make.

Here's how:

1) Cut the two fabric halves and put them face to face. If you plan to put in a zipper, sew it to the pieces first (follow the directions on the package).

2) Stitch the fabric together along three sides about ½" in from the edges.

3) Trim off excess seam allowance and turn the cover right side out. Stuff the cover.

4) If you didn't put in a zipper, slipstitch the opening closed.

1) put fabric's finished sides face to face

2) stitch ½" from edges / opening / stitch around corner

3) turn right side out and stuff with foam

4) close opening with overcast stitch

**Box cushions.** Box-shaped cushions have side panels that help maintain their rectangular shape. One is shown below. They're harder to make than knife-edge cushions.

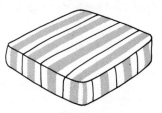

BOX CUSHION

Here's how:

1) Cut out the six pieces, allowing for a ½" seam allowance around all edges.

2) Install a zipper in one of the side panels (or figure for a similar closure).

3) Working on the wrong sides of the fabric, sew the four side panels together end to end, allowing about ½" seams.

4) Sew the side panels to the top and bottom panels. Trim excess allowances.

5) Turn the cover right side out and fill it.

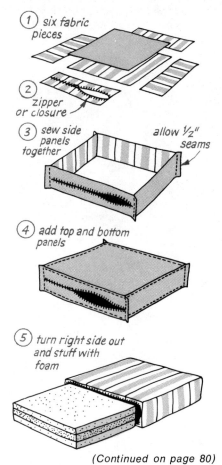

1) six fabric pieces

2) zipper or closure

3) sew side panels together / allow ½" seams

4) add top and bottom panels

5) turn right side out and stuff with foam

(Continued on page 80)

. . . Continued from page 79

**Drawstring covers.** Bolsters and other round-form cushions—like the caterpillar lounge cushions on page 7, the inner-tube chairs on page 18, and the green easy chair on page 31 — can be covered with drawstring covers. These are very easy to make.

Here's how:

1) Cut the fabric to fit the shape (see more about sizing fabric in the description of making the inner-tube covers on page 21).

2) For a cover open at only one end, first make a knife-edge cushion cover, as described on page 79. For a cover open at both ends, seam the two ends of the fabric together, forming a cylinder that fits the cushion shape, and press the seam open.

3) Make the casings for the drawstrings at one or both ends by folding the fabric's edges over twice and stitching along the first fold (leave a ½" opening for the drawstring). See drawing 80-2.

4) Fasten a safety pin onto one end of the drawstring and fish it through the casing. Adjust the cord evenly once it's through. Tie a knot in each end.

5) Turn the cover right side out, slip it over the cylinder or stuffing, and pull the cord taut, gathering the fabric evenly. Tie the ends together and tuck them in the opening.

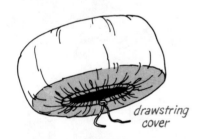

drawstring cover

DRAWING 80-1

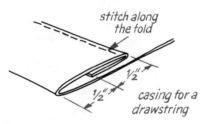

stitch along the fold

½"

½"

casing for a drawstring

DRAWING 80-2

**Irregularly shaped cushions.** To cover cushions of unusual shapes, follow the instructions for box or knife-edge cushions. Make a paper pattern to fit the dimensions of the cushion form. To insure accuracy, test the pattern by making a sample cover from muslin or fabric scraps.

**Mitered corners** (for knife-edge cushions). You can add a bit more distinction to knife-edge cushions by mitering the corners (see drawing

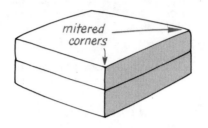

mitered corners

DRAWING 80-3

80-3). Here are two ways it can be done:

1) When the cover is inside out and stitched, fold it so the seams are centered on top of each other and

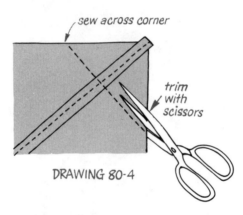

sew across corner

trim with scissors

DRAWING 80-4

pin the corners. Make the miter by sewing across the corners, perpendicular to the seam lines, 1½" to 3½" in from the edges. (The resulting triangle will determine the cushion's depth.) Trim the corner to eliminate bulk in the seam.

2) A folded miter can be made after sewing the cushion cover and turning it right side out. Simply fold the corner inside to make a neat pocket. Because sewing through several thicknesses is difficult, this works best for bulky fabrics and leathers. The couch on page 15 has folded miter cushions.

**Closing a cushion's opening**

As previously mentioned, you have to decide early how you'll close the opening that you push the stuffing through. Install zippers and similar devices according to the directions on the package. If you're inexperienced, putting them in can be difficult; here are a couple of alternatives.

A simple solution is to allow extra fabric at the cushion's backside. From this fabric, make two overlapping fabric panels. Hem and overlap the two pieces 1½" to 3" before stuffing the cushion.

The easiest way to close a cushion is to handstitch the last seam. Of course, to remove the cover, you have to cut the seam open. The overcast stitch, shown in drawing 80-5, is strong, fast, and easy to master.

Another permanent closure is machine topstitching. After the cover is turned right side out and stuffed, fold in the raw edges of the unfinished seam and stitch both together, close to the edge, with a short machine stitch.

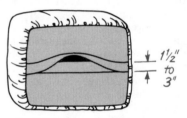

1½" to 3"

extra fabric at cushion's backside overlaps for an easy-to-make closure

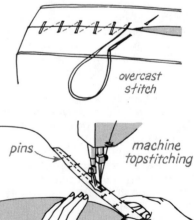

overcast stitch

pins

machine topstitching

DRAWING 80-5